CRITICAL TERMS FOR SCIENCE FICTION AND FANTASY

CRITICAL TERMS FOR SCIENCE FICTION AND FANTASY

A Glossary and Guide to Scholarship

Gary K. Wolfe

GREENWOOD PRESS
New York
Westport, Connecticut
London

Library of Congress Cataloging-in-Publication Data

Wolfe, Gary K., 1946-
  Critical terms for science fiction and fantasy.

  Bibliography: p.
  Includes index.
    1. Fantastic fiction—Dictionaries.   2. Science
fiction—Dictionaries.   3. Criticism—Dictionaries.
I. Title.
PN3435.W64   1986   809.3′876   86-3138
ISBN 0-313-22981-3 (lib. bdg. : alk. paper)

Library of Congress Catalog Card Number: 86-3138
ISBN: 0-313-22981-3

First published in 1986

Greenwood Press, Inc.
88 Post Road West, Westport, Connecticut 06881

Printed in the United States of America

The paper used in this book complies with the
Permanent Paper Standard issued by the National
Information Standards Organization (Z39.48-1984).

10 9 8 7 6 5 4 3 2 1

Contents

Preface

For perhaps half a century now, those who write and read (and write about) science fiction have been chronically unable to agree upon even the meaning of the term "science fiction" itself. In more recent years, similar debates have arisen regarding allied genres of fantastic literature, such as fantasy or horror fiction. Such confusion over the most basic terminology is only the most visible symptom of a growing problem that is apparent to anyone who reads widely in the criticism and history of these kinds of literature: On the one hand, concepts from traditional literary discourse often seem inadequate to describe the peculiar techniques and effects of the fantastic, while, on the other, terms coined specifically to describe such literature frequently appear eccentric or esoteric. Few branches of modern literary study have yielded as many neologisms, specialized definitions, attempts at identifying subgenres, and appropriations from other scholarly vocabularies as has the study of fantastic literature—and yet the field is still far too young to have established anything resembling a consensus critical vocabulary.

This glossary—the first literary glossary devoted specifically to the study of fantastic literature—is not an attempt to prescribe such a vocabulary, but rather to provide a guide to the breadth and variety of the critical thought that has been brought to bear on this field. Nor is this an encyclopedic reference work devoted to listing authors or themes— several such works are available, and many are included in the bibliography. (I would especially recommend Peter Nicholls' *Science Fiction Encyclopedia* [1979] for those interested in such a comprehensive work.) Finally, it is not a guide to that unique and colorful specialized vocabulary known as "fanspeak," which is covered in Wilson Tucker's "Neofan's Guide" (1955, 1973). Furthermore, this work contains very few terms that overlap with such previous works.

A word of explanation is in order, then: What, exactly, is this book for? Of the nearly 500 terms listed, most are drawn from critical books and essays specifically concerned with science fiction and fantasy—both from academic critics and from others who have written significantly about these kinds of literature—especially practicing authors. Some of these terms, like "extrapolation," entered the critical vocabulary through a gradual process of assimilation. Others, such as "speculative fiction" or "cognitive estrangement," have been specifically suggested by particular authors or critics. Unless such terms happen to gain unusually wide acceptance, they are not likely to show up in standard reference works, even though they may provide useful ways of thinking about fantastic literature.

Another sizable group of terms (for example, "romance") comes from the standard vocabulary of scholarly discourse, primarily that of literary study but occasionally from such related fields as psychology or anthropology. These terms have been included only when they have been appropriated for specific uses by writers about fantastic literature, or when they represent attitudes toward such literature by significant "mainstream" critics. Still other terms, like "blurb," may come from the publishing industry itself, which is inevitably closely involved with the development of any popular literature, and which has on occasion lent special meaning to terms that later show up in critical and historical vocabularies. Finally, there are a few fan terms, which have been included only when they have entered broader critical usage than that represented by the fan community itself.

Some thematic terms are included, particularly those that have been used to refer to a particular set of conventions or subgenre and that are not self-explanatory. Thus, while it did not seem necessary to include "time travel," which is a fairly ubiquitous concept in a wide variety of works, "post-holocaust" is included because of specific historical and generic meanings that have been attached to it. Neologisms that are themselves part of a science fiction narrative—such as A. E. Van Vogt's "nexialism" or Jack Williamson's "seetee"—are generally excluded, although Isaac Asimov's "psychohistory" shows up, because of its frequent confusion with the later concept as used by historians and because of its significant relationship to ideas of cyclical history that have often been invoked in discussing science fiction. Similarly, Asimov's "laws of robotics" is included because of the extent to which it has generated critical debate that goes far beyond the specific stories that introduced the concept. There is no entry for "robot," however.

Since the terms included were derived from scores of writings about science fiction and fantasy ranging over more than a century and a half, it seemed necessary to attempt to establish a context for them by providing some historical background. The introductory essay, then, tries to identify some of the major conceptual problems that have evolved in discussions of fantastic literature and to show how these problems have in part been exacerbated by the development of separate critical traditions in England and America and among the various groups who have written about this literature—including authors, fans, publishers, academic students of the genre, and "mainstream" critics. One hears the complaint that science fiction too often singles itself out for special consideration apart from the "mainstream," and indeed the very existence of a work such as this might seem to reinforce that self-imposed segregation. But the fact remains that, whatever the causes, the critical vocabulary of the mainstream often gives short shrift to the fantastic, and scholars of the fantastic have often had to look elsewhere for their critical terminology.

This work began as part of what was to have been a larger volume confined to fantasy literature. An attempt at compiling a short glossary of important critical terms, however, soon led me into a morass of conflicting definitions and concepts, and the research involved in tracking down some of these terms grew increasingly challenging and fascinating. Some of the entries, in fact, turned into short essays in attempts to pin down the significance of particular concepts, while others turned into mini-anthologies. (So many definitions of "science fiction" and "fantasy" turned up, for example, that it would have seemed the height of hubris to try to synthesize these without letting other critics speak for themselves.) It began to seem apparent that the glossary would likely be the most fascinating part of the book. Finally, expanded to include terms for science fiction as well as fantasy, it became *the* book. The bibliography, which follows the glossary and to which entries in the glossary are keyed, includes works important for their first or subsequent usages of the terms defined and is in no sense supposed to be definitive. Those seeking critical bibliographies are urged instead to consult such works as Thomas D. Clareson's *Science Fiction Criticism: An Annotated Checklist* (1972); Marshall B. Tymn, Roger C. Schlobin, and L. W. Currey's *A Research Guide to Science Fiction Studies* (1977); and Marshall B. Tymn and Roger C. Schlobin's *The Year's Scholarship in Science Fiction and Fantasy* (1979 and subsequent years).

Roger Schlobin shared his considerable expertise about fantasy with me throughout much of the project. Algis Budrys, who probably needs this volume less than the rest of us, shared at times his encyclopedic recall and critical acuity (and was himself the source of several terms). Russell Letson also steered me toward some unusual terms and usages and let me read his essay on academics and fans which proved invaluable in preparing the introduction. Catherine McClenahan read part of the manuscript and insightfully pointed out incomplete or (worse) "copout" attempts at definition. Finally, I should thank Greenwood Press and Marilyn Brownstein in particular for a remarkable display of patience as this thing remained in its cocoon stage for an unconscionable length of time, before finally transforming into something other than what it was supposed to be in the first place. (My wife, Kary, also endured this period.) Needless to say, none of these people bear any responsibility for errors or misrepresentations that may be present—nor do any of the scores of scholars and theorists about fantastic literature whose work and thought make up the substance of this volume, and to whom it is dedicated.

Introduction: Fantastic Literature and Literary Discourse

The relationship between the arts of fantastic literature and the arts of scholarly inquiry has long been a vaguely distrustful one; some might even characterize it as a marriage of convenience born out of the science fiction or fantasy writer's yearning for acceptance in the literary community and the academic's need for fresh critical material and improved enrollments in sagging literature classes. To a great extent, in fact, the dramatic blossoming of science fiction and fantasy scholarship which began in the mid–1970s has been an extended game of catch-up: Students (and teachers) from the thousand-odd science fiction and fantasy classes suddenly being taught on campuses all over the world besieged librarians for basic reference material, only to find that even the most respected of genre authors were excluded from standard literary reference works. The resulting demand created a significant library market for reference works, books on the teaching of fantastic genres, general guides or introductions to these genres, and more theoretical critical and historical studies. At the same time, the growing acceptance of the genres as objects of formal scholarly scrutiny created an atmosphere amenable to critical dialogue within the academic community, and the community of fans and professional authors continued as always to express a keen interest in the nature and background of their field, as well as interest in details about specific authors, publications, and works.

Science fiction and fantasy critics and scholars—most originally trained in other academic fields—responded to this demand with a vengeance, and genres that only a few years earlier had been all but invisible in scholarly journals and on library reference shelves suddenly were among the most scrutinized, catalogued, anatomized, and cross-referenced phenomena in modern literature. Three major scholarly journals—*Extrapolation*, *Science-Fiction Studies*, and *Foundation*—appeared between 1959 and 1972, and existing "fanzines" such as *Riverside Quarterly* turned increasingly toward academic content. Reference works, once the sole province of the fan press, began to appear from established publishers for the library market during the 1970s, each one, it seemed, more ambitious than the last. (The culmination of this exploitation of the library market may well have been the Salem Press *Surveys* of science fiction and fantasy, which appeared in 1979 and 1983 with a combined total of over 5,000 pages of critical commentary!) Histories and theoretical studies began to proliferate, as did extensive bibliographies not only of "classic," but of currently active authors. Series of individual author studies appeared both from small presses such as Starmont House and from major academic houses such as Oxford University Press, while familiar ongoing series (such as those from Twayne) began for the first time to include substantial numbers of volumes dealing with authors of the fantastic. The collection of critical essays, usually a relatively minor factor in the scholarship of more traditional literary fields, became a dominant outlet for the scholarship of science fiction and fantasy, to the extent that in 1982, more original essays appeared in such volumes than in all the scholarly journals in the field combined. (Ironically, this seems to parallel the history of science fiction book publishing, which was largely dominated by anthologies during the postwar years before the novel established its own market.)

While many of these works were excellent by any standards, others were hastily produced and seemed to give credence to fears within the science fiction and fantasy community that academia was after all opportunistic and exploitative, that academics were less interested in doing serious research in the field than in seeking tenure in a contracting profession. Such concerns were expressed repeatedly during the 1970s not only by fans, but by professional writers and editors including Lloyd Biggle, Jr., William Tenn, and Lester del Rey. While their fears that the involvement of academia might somehow do "damage" to science fiction itself seem rather naive, some of the specific concerns they expressed were not entirely without foundation, and the argument can be made that academic publishing standards in science fiction and fantasy have indeed become less rigorous than in some other scholarly areas. (Again, it is tempting to draw a parallel with the history of science fiction itself, and its period of pulp magazines during which prolificacy was encouraged and deadlines were always imminent.) The extreme statement of this position was made by Algis Budrys in a now-famous and controversial review in the January 1983 *Magazine of Fantasy and Science Fiction*, where he stated flatly that "the formal scholarship of speculative fiction is, taken in the whole, worthless."[1] In addition to accusing academics of being intellectually incestuous and of not doing adequate primary research in the field, Budrys made an interesting point regarding an essay by Harold Bloom in the volume under review. Quoting a passage from Bloom, Budrys claimed it was "not directed at anyone outside a tight circle who all share the same vocabulary and the same library." The would-be literary scholar, Budrys argued, is forced to read more criticism than actual literature, or would be in danger of losing "his grip on the nomenclature."

Budrys's point may be exaggerated, and the passage from Bloom that prompted it may indeed seem arcane with its allusions to little-known Gnostic writers, but the complaint has been made by academics themselves—both in and out of the science fiction and fantasy field—that scholarship and what passes for scholarship have proliferated almost out of control, that there are few established standards for such scholarship, and that the plethora of opportunities for publications and conference papers does in fact come to look suspiciously like a kind of "tenure machine" for junior faculty. Far from being the "tight circle" of initiates that Budrys suspects, scholarship of the fantastic more often resembles an intellectual flea market, with various methodologies, values, definitions, and even primary texts competing for the attention of scholars from disparate backgrounds who so far have not even been quite able to agree upon what it is they are talking about.

Thus the main issue that Budrys raises in his complaint about audience and vocabulary is one that bibliographer and editor Everett F. Bleiler reiterated in his acceptance address for the 1984 Pilgrim Award from the Science Fiction Research Association. "Our terms have become muddled, imprecise, and heretical in the derivational sense of the word," Bleiler wrote.[2] Even such ubiquitous terms as "science fiction," "fantasy," "Gothic," and "utopia" lack commonly accepted meanings, he argued, and anyone undertaking extended reading in this area of scholarship would be compelled to agree with him. At times it seems as though every author of a theoretical or critical study deems it necessary to invent terms or assign new definitions to old ones as a means of staking a claim to originality, and these new definitions often in turn imply whole new taxonomies or critical structures. At its most confusing, the situation resembles what R. D. Mullen, in a 1976 review, characterized as "Every Critic His Own Aristotle."[3] No one is quite certain whether "the fantastic" describes a group of texts, something that happens within a text (or at what level it happens), or something that happens to the reader encountering the text. Much the same is true of science fiction. There is not even much agreement as to which texts ought to be discussed. While scholars trained in literary disciplines gravitate toward those works that most resemble those they have been trained to read (J. R. R. Tolkien and C. S. Lewis for several years accounted for nearly a sixth of *all* the scholarly studies written about science fiction or fantasy authors), fans may gravitate toward those works that most epitomize what they like to read. Those whose point of reference is Robert A. Heinlein may well question the relevance to science fiction of an essay on the political ambiguities of Ursula K. Le Guin, while those who come to science fiction via the "literariness" of Le Guin are apt to be mightily puzzled when they encounter A. E. Van Vogt.

Part of the reason for this confusion is that the vocabulary of modern science fiction and fantasy studies derives from a number of different traditions of discourse. I am not referring here to the "two cultures" argument or to the often-stated belief among many science fiction writers that proper discussion of the genre requires mastery of science as well as of literature; if anything, this alleged problem has long since given way to overcompensation, with humanistically trained scholars taking obvious pride in their ability to invoke the vocabularies of science and writers or fans equally resolute in demonstrating their mastery of traditional literary concepts. The problems involved in establishing a coherent domain of discourse are not likely to be resolved by science fiction or fantasy writers talking ever more loudly about Balzac's narrative structures or Faulkner's style, or by literary critics and scholars summarizing for their own benefit the enigmas of quantum mechanics and radio astronomy. Certainly, the dialogue between the sciences and humanities that such things may lead to is commendable, but little if any of the present confusion about terminology derives from such a schism.

The problem is not that the language of the literature differs from the language of scholarly analysis—that problem is hardly unique to science fiction and fantasy—but that separate ways of writing about fantastic literature have evolved quite apart from each other, each with its particular claim to precision and validity, and each contributing piecemeal to the growth of a critical vocabulary. Concepts evolved in fandom, in commercial publishing, in traditions of scholarship devoted principally to realistic literature have met up with terms from the social sciences and from such interdisciplinary domains as myth study, semiotics, popular culture, and structuralism. A second factor adding to this confusion is that science fiction scholarship has, with few exceptions, evolved along slightly different paths from fantasy scholarship, even though these traditions increasingly need to speak to each other about works they have in common as well as about common methodological and theoretical problems. Finally—and this is specifically the "every critic his own Aristotle" problem—any emerging field of study is likely to yield an inordinate number of neologisms as critics and scholars, finding little in the way of background research or consensus terminology, simply concoct their own terms and concepts to help organize and clarify their arguments. I doubt that any such critic is deliberately trying to be obtuse, but when enough follow this practice, a point of diminishing returns is soon reached at which the development of a common domain of discourse is threatened rather than advanced. The problem is not unique to science fiction and fantasy study by any means; it can be seen and demonstrated in such highly methodological fields as semiotics and in other areas of popular culture scholarship such as film or television study.

The result, of course, is some suspicion on all fronts. Scholars complain that terms from fandom, such as "extrapolation" or "sense of wonder," are imprecise and faddish, while fans and writers complain that academics write only for each other. A publishing term such as "pulp" confusingly may refer to a kind of cheap paper stock, the prose printed on it, the assumptions underlying that prose, or any authors (even of the modern era) who partake of those assumptions. A term such as this may also carry widely varying connotations: for a fan writer, "pulp" may invoke a "Golden Age" (another rubbery term), while to a traditional scholar, it may refer to one of the genre's worst embarrassments. "Myth" may mean a specific mechanism of cultural organization to one group of scholars or a primitive story to another; for some fans it might be a buzzword to invoke cultural legitimacy for a favorite genre. Each group, of course, claims to be speaking English while the others are hopelessly mired in jargon.

IMAGINATION AND FANCY

Of these various domains of discourse that we employ to talk about science fiction and fantasy, probably the first to evolve was the vocabulary of imagination and fancy, familiar to modern readers from its most famous formulation in Samuel Taylor Coleridge's *Biographia Literaria* in 1817. But the debate over these terms had been going on for more than a century prior to Coleridge's essay. In 1712, Joseph Addison wrote, "There are few words in the English language which are employed in a more loose and uncircumscribed sense than those of the fancy and the imagination."[4] In setting out "to fix and determine the notion of these two words," however, Addison made it clear that both originally derive from sight. In other words, what we call imagination or fancy has to do with our reactions to or memories of objects of nature or art. Addison's view partakes of what was already a long-standing view of imagination as a "mirror" of the external world, to use a metaphor from Yeats borrowed by M. H. Abrams in his classic 1953 study, *The Mirror and the Lamp*. But within the next century or so, this view of imagination, thanks largely to the Romantic movement, would come to be supplanted by a view of imagination as a "lamp" illuminating unseen worlds beyond perceived reality.

This new view was already in evidence by the mid-eighteenth century.

In 1741, the German critic, poet, and translator of Milton's *Paradise Lost*, Johann Jakob Bodmer, wrote:

The imagination is not merely the soul's treasury, where the senses store their pictures in safe-keeping for subsequent use; besides this it also has a region of its own which extends much further than the dimension of the senses. . . . It not only places the real before our eyes in a vivid image and makes distant things present, but also, with a power more potent than that of magic, it draws that which does not exist out of the state of potentiality, gives it a semblance of reality and makes us see, hear and feel these new creations.[5]

By 1762, a similar definition of imagination had entered the English language, with Lord Henry Home Kames writing in his *Elements of Criticism*, "this singular power of fabricating images without any foundation in reality is distinguished by the name of *imagination*."[6]

A number of literary historians have identified this shift in the theory of imagination as a revolution, a fundamental break in the history of critical thought. It led, predictably enough, to a new attitude toward the fantastic (which Friedrich Schlegel claimed in 1800 was a defining characteristic of Romantic literature), and in turn to a number of debates about the proper uses of the fantastic and the relative merits of images drawn from nature, and images that sought to go beyond nature. The brothers A. W. and Friedrich Schlegel, for example, devoted much of their journal, *Das Athenaeum*, from 1798 to 1800 to debates about the rules of fairy tales and other forms of Romantic literature. In his 1810 "A Vision of the Last Judgment," William Blake equated imagination with "Visionary Fancy" and set this apart from fable or allegory, "a totally distinct & inferior kind of Poetry . . . Fable or Allegory is Form'd by the daughters of Memory. Imagination is surrounded by the daughters of Inspiration. . . . "[7] Blake's distinction not only anticipates Coleridge (albeit with a different set of terms), but also anticipates a critical battle that authors of fantasy from George MacDonald to C. S. Lewis would wage—namely, that fantastic narratives are not necessarily allegories or fables.

But it was Samuel Taylor Coleridge's 1817 distinction between fancy and imagination that set the stage for the critical debate that would occupy much of the nineteenth century and that arguably surrounded the birth of the modern fantasy narrative. Writing in the early chapters of *Biographia Literaria* about Wordsworth's poetry, Coleridge describes his growing conviction "that fancy and imagination were two distinct and widely different faculties, instead of being, according to the general belief, either two names with one meaning, or, at furthest, the lower and higher degree of one and the same power."[8] Later he describes the imagination as "the living Power and prime Agent of all human Perception," the most godlike of human qualities, while the fancy "has no other counters to to play with, but fixities and definites. The Fancy is indeed no other than a mode of Memory emancipated from the order of time and space. . . . "[9] In other words, the earlier concept of imagination—that it is essentially a mode of memory—Coleridge relegates to the secondary status of "fancy," while the imagination represents something new and entirely different—what Coleridge was to call (in a term that fortunately has not gained wide acceptance) the "esemplastic" power of the mind.

In English literary discourse, Coleridge's famous distinction did much to establish the terms by which fantastic literature would be discussed for the rest of the century, and in so doing, to give legitimacy to the notion of a vocabulary of the fantastic. Indeed, according to Stephen Prickett, "by 1825 something very extraordinary had happened. From being terms of derision, or descriptions of daydreaming, words like 'fantasy' and 'imagination' suddenly began to take on new status as hurrah-words."[10] But while Romantic poets and their critics could undertake debates about the nature of imagination as revealed through literary art, and while Romantic narrative artists such as Edgar Allan Poe and Sir Walter Scott could begin to construct theoretical examinations of the nature of their craft (a tradition continued by later fantastic authors from George MacDonald to J. R. R. Tolkien and C. S. Lewis), critics in the major English journals remained skeptical of the uses of the fantastic in works of fiction.[11] Fantasy elements were widely regarded as superstitious and were generally tolerated only if supported by evidence of actual belief or if supported by didactic or moral purpose. Even Sir Walter Scott himself, while praising Mary Shelley's *Frankenstein* (1818) in his essay "On the Supernatural in Fictitious Composition" (1827), demanded that fantastic elements should be controlled and characterized by "philosophical reasoning and moral truth."[12] Scott's essay is of interest not only because it represents one of the earliest critical discussions of a work now generally regarded as science fiction, but because it reveals an attitude that would become increasingly dominant in the later nineteenth century: that fantastic inventions, in an increasingly pragmatic and industrialized age, required some sort of extraliterary rationale for their legitimate employment in a work of literature.

The attitude is exemplified in a more extreme form in an anonymous essay titled "The Progress of Fiction as an Art," which appeared in the *Westminster Review* in 1853. Argued this author, art, like technology, progresses from more primitive to more sophisticated forms, and "a scientific, and somewhat sceptical age, has no longer the power of believing in the marvels which delighted our ruder ancestors."[13] The fantastic, in other words, was inappropriate for an age of science and morality, and the values of realism came to dominate literary discourse, despite the fact that the Victorian age itself was one of the great periods in the development of fantasy literature. "Falsehood is so easy, truth so difficult," wrote George Eliot in 1859. "The pencil is conscious of a delightful facility in drawing a griffin—the longer the claws, and the larger the wings, the better; but that marvellous facility which we mistook for genius is apt to forsake us when we want to draw a real unexaggerated lion."[14]

THE DEFENSE OF FANTASY

Realism became not only a principle of the journal reviewers of nineteenth-century England and America, but also one of the early values inculcated in the formalized study of literature in the classroom. It is important to remember that a critical vocabulary for the discussion of works of fiction did not really emerge until the universities began to accept fiction as worthy of formal scrutiny, and that universities by and large resisted this until well into the twentieth century. As an academic discipline, "English" began as a working-class version of classics studies, "first institutionalized," as Terry Eagleton writes, "not in the Universities, but in the Mechanics' Institutes, working men's colleges and extension lecturing circuits."[15] (It is important for scholars and writers especially of science fiction to remember, in their dismay over the reluctance of traditional departments to accept their subject as a valid scholarly endeavor, that similar battles were once fought for English literature, American literature, and, more recently, film—not to mention such other areas as anthropology, sociology, and economics.) The study of vernacular literature was thus viewed as a kind of moral imperative, focusing on the humanizing and "improving" effects such literature might have on those who studied it; this factor, too, undoubtedly helped shift the focus of literary discourse toward realism and representations of actual life.

Partly for these reasons, when something reasonably resembling modern fantasy began to emerge, it often did so in the disguise of children's literature (as with Carroll and Kingsley), pseudohistorical fiction (as with Scott), or pseudomedievalia (as with Morris). And for similar reasons, critical discussions of fantasy have often been primarily defenses of the genre. In fact, it might be argued that much modern fantasy theory derives from this externally motivated rhetorical stance. When an early reviewer of George MacDonald's *Phantastes* (1858), sometimes regarded as the first modern fantasy novel in English (although heavily derivative of German *Kunstmärchen*), treated the book as an allegory, MacDonald fired off a rather impatient letter to a friend, complaining, "I don't see what right the *Athenaeum* has to call it an allegory and judge or misjudge it accordingly—as if nothing but an allegory could

have two meanings!"[16] The resurrection of Blake's old distinction between allegorical and visionary imagination became a recurring necessity
in fantasy criticism, and it quickly became conflated with Coleridge's
distinction between fancy and imagination. In his 1893 essay "The Fantastic Imagination," MacDonald offered his own definitions of these
terms, arguing (as one might expect from a Scottish minister) that the
higher faculty of imagination represents "new embodiments of old truths,"
whereas fancy consists merely of invention for its own sake.[17]

Among the "old truths" that MacDonald referred to was the notion
that the physical universe might yield to moral laws, a notion increasingly
embattled under the discoveries of Victorian science, but one that could
be safely reclaimed in the context of a fantastic narrative. Several early
writers about fantasy expressed such ideas. G. K. Chesterton, for example, in his 1908 essay "The Ethics of Elfland," defended fairy tales
according to what he called a "Doctrine of Conditional Joy"—the notion, common in fairy tales, that a great reward might depend on not
violating some apparently arbitrary taboo, thus implying a universe governed by human actions rather than by coldly mechanistic forces. Such
a universe, of course, may be found in myth, and it was not long before
critics of fantasy would turn to myth as an appropriate narrative model
(and a source of legitimacy) for fantastic narratives. E. M. Forster's
1927 *Aspects of the Novel* includes a chapter on what he called the
"fantastic-prophetical axis" of fiction—works that convey a sense of
mythic time or that imply the presence of a supernatural world—and
defines an important subgenre that connects such works to mythic sources,
namely the "adaptation" or reworking of familiar classical material.

MODERN FANTASY THEORY

Despite the frequent defenses of the genre by MacDonald, Chesterton, and others such as Oscar Wilde and William Morris, it can be
argued that much of modern academic scholarship of fantasy derives
from one essay. In 1938, while he was working on the trilogy that would
perhaps do more than any other single work to place fantasy study in
the university curriculum (for better or worse), the Oxford philologist
J. R. R. Tolkien delivered a lecture titled "On Fairy-Stories" at the
University of St. Andrews. Later expanded for inclusion in an Oxford
University Press volume in honor of Tolkien's friend Charles Williams,
this lecture outlined a number of concepts that have since become staples
in fantasy theory. Beginning by attempting to define (largely by exclu-
sion) the fairy story, Tolkien soon focuses on the term "Faerie" itself,
identifying this as the "Perilous Realm," the general details of atmosphere and setting that reveal a sense of the supernatural, a magical view
of nature, and a "Mirror of scorn and pity" toward humanity. Such a

"secondary world" demands literary or "secondary belief," and the artist who creates such a world becomes, on the model of the deity, a "sub-creator."[18]

Such fantasy, argues Tolkien, offers four principal psychological functions for the reader. Fantasy itself is the first of these—the purest form of human creativity, and one that enhances rather than undermines reason, since it depends on the reader's exercise in distinguishing the real from the not-real. "Recovery" is Tolkien's term for the "regaining of a clear view" or an innocent perspective; and "escape" is a kind of coping mechanism exemplified by the symbolic escape from death embodied in many fairy stories. Finally, "consolation" is provided by the tale's happy ending, or "eucatastrophe." Overall, these effects give rise to a sense of "joy" not unlike the joy of religious revelation. (Tolkien even suggests the Gospels as a kind of mythic model for the fairy tale form.) A later psychoanalytic critic, Bruno Bettelheim, adopted Tolkien's four-part reader-response structure in his 1976 study, *The Uses of Enchantment*.

The same volume of *Essays Presented to Charles Williams* in which "On Fairy-Stories" first saw print also included a shorter essay by Tolkien's fellow-Inkling, C. S. Lewis. Lewis's famous "space trilogy" (*Out of the Silent Planet*, 1938; *Perelandra*, 1943; *That Hideous Strength*, 1945) had given him what was at the time a wider reputation as a fantasist than Tolkien's, and his still-earlier classic study of medieval narrative tradition (*The Allegory of Love*, 1936) had laid out a number of ideas that would become crucial to modern approaches to fantasy. George MacDonald's anger at being called an allegorist was indirectly reflected in that volume, for example, when Lewis distinguishes between allegorical and "symbolic" narratives, the latter symbolizing aspects of a higher reality rather than aspects of the experiential world. Lewis also traced the gradual "liberation" of fantasy narratives from their allegorical justifications, giving rise to stories in which the imagination becomes largely its own reward.

"On Stories," which appeared in the Oxford University Press volume, carried this argument further by postulating that "story" serves a liberating function quite apart from its embodiment in a particular rhetorical mode, and citing fantasy as the purest form of storytelling. More than Tolkien, Lewis brought his ideas to bear on works that have since come to be regarded as part of the canon of modern fantasy—William Morris' *The Well at the World's End* (1896), David Lindsay's *A Voyage to Arcturus* (1920), E. R. Eddison's *The Worm Ouroboros* (1922)—and thus helped to establish that canon as well. In later essays, Lewis defended fantasy in the context of his own fiction, of children's literature, and of science fiction (although he came to view the latter as a kind of mechanistic degradation of mythic storytelling). His 1961 *An Experiment in Criticism*—the "experiment" was his suggestion to suspend evaluative criticism for a while and let reader response dictate the relative power of works of literature—included chapters on myth, fantasy, and realism. Myth he viewed as the most powerful of all stories, not only because of its numinous quality but because of its extraliterary appeal, its sense of inevitability, and its fantastic elements. Fantasy and realism, he argued, are both confusing and misused terms—fantasy because of its various psychological and cultural meanings, realism because it may refer either to "realism of content" (verisimilitude) or "realism of presentation" (internal consistency and believability).

In 1961, when *An Experiment in Criticism* appeared, there was still no coherent body of academic work on fantasy. Occasional essays had appeared in specialized journals, a few authors such as Morris had been treated as part of Victorian studies, and several studies of children's literature had found it necessary to deal with fantasy; but as a genre fantasy had received not even the attention paid to the Gothic horror story. During the 1960s, however, two developments drew the attention of the academic world to fantasy, or at least to the fantastic. One was the enormous popular success, especially on college campuses, of Tolkien's *Lord of the Rings* trilogy in its Ballantine paperback edition. The other was the employment of fantastic themes and images on the part of a number of major literary figures such as John Barth, Vladimir Nabokov, Jorge Luis Borges, and Thomas Pynchon. Other factors may have also played a role in bringing about increased attention to the fantastic—the growing popularity of science fiction, new attention being paid to popular literature and popular culture in general, a shift toward structural and analytical rather than historical and evaluative modes of criticism—even, some would say, the depletion of fertile ground for younger academics seeking a route to tenure or a dissertation topic.

Certainly, the interaction of Anglo-American and European modes of criticism became a factor. One of the first systematic theoretical works to deal with fantastic literature was Bulgarian philologist Tzvetan Todorov's *The Fantastic: A Structural Approach to a Literary Genre* (1970), which appeared in English translation in 1973. Todorov's dual purpose of critiquing genre theory and defining the structure of a particular genre called attention to the ways in which fantastic literature raises important questions about narrative in general, and helped to bring the fantastic to the attention of other literary theorists. The fantastic, according to Todorov, must satisfy three conditions: It should establish a believable narrative world in which events occur that cause the reader to hesitate between natural and supernatural explanations; it should provide a viewpoint character who shares this hesitation; and it should steer the reader away from purely poetic or allegorical interpretations of these events. Once this hesitation is resolved and the fantastic events prove real or unreal, the work moves into another genre: the "uncanny," or super-natural explained, or the "marvelous." While many students of fantasy find this definition of a genre unacceptably narrow (much fantasy would seem to fit into Todorov's category of the marvelous), Todorov does go on to offer a number of important comments on the nature of the marvelous and the ways in which it might be manipulated through various techniques. Science fiction, for example, is the "scientific marvel-ous," in which objects impossible in the world of the narrative are rationalized through scientific or pseudoscientific means.

By shifting the discussion of the fantastic away from purely thematic or topical considerations and toward the state of mind of the reader, Todorov invited a kind of rhetorical criticism of fantasy that quickly became a central element in modern discussions of the genre. Of those studies written largely or in part in response to Todorov, the most significant is surely Rosemary Jackson's *Fantasy: The Literature of Subversion* (1981). Viewing fantasy as a somewhat broader literary mode than does Todorov, Jackson brings to its study a number of concepts from psychoanalytic theory, arguing that fantasy is a historically determined form which provides expression for the fundamental anxieties and desires of a culture.

Eric S. Rabkin's *The Fantastic in Literature* (1976) owes some debts to Todorov but takes a radically different approach to the idea of the fantastic. Whereas Todorov focuses on a particular element within a work which might make it fantastic, Rabkin defines the fantastic as a broad continuum of works ranging from the nearly realistic to the purely chaotic and dreamlike. Science fiction, myths, fairy tales, horror stories, heroic fantasy, and many other genres may be arrayed along this continuum according to their fantastic content. What defines fantasy, he argues, is the deliberate reversal of "ground rules" within the narrative and the depiction of events that are later shown to be in keeping with the new ground rules; Rabkin calls such events "dis-expected" as opposed to "unexpected." Like Tolkien and Lewis, Rabkin defends the escapist function of such works by arguing that they may offer new perspectives on the reader's experiential world, that they may reveal new modes of perception, and that in fact the fantastic may collectively constitute a "basic mode of human knowing."[19]

The same year that Rabkin's study appeared saw the publication of W. R. Irwin's *The Game of the Impossible: A Rhetoric of Fantasy*. Broader in focus than Todorov's and yet narrower than Rabkin's, Irwin's study was perhaps the first to attempt a formal delineation of a genre of fantasy, which he defined as "a story based on and controlled by an overt violation of what is generally accepted as possibility."[20] While this bears obvious similarities to Rabkin's reversal of "ground rules," Irwin adds the dimension of "play" in arguing that this violation of norms is willingly participated in as a kind of "conspiracy" between author and reader. Irwin identifies five types of fantasy—those involving supernatural powers, those based on impossible personal changes or metamorphoses, those dealing with incredible societies, those that adapt or parody other works or belief systems, and those based on "organized innocence" or childlike simplicity. Unlike Rabkin, however, he concludes that fantasy is finally a diversion, based in wit, play, and fancy, and not a part of the mainstream traditions of human thought or literature.

A similar conclusion is reached by the Scottish critic C. N. Manlove in his 1975 *Modern Fantasy: Five Studies*. After defining fantasy as fiction evoking wonder and centrally involving supernatural beings, things, or worlds, Manlove draws a distinction similar to that drawn by George MacDonald between fancy and imagination. MacDonald's "fancy" here becomes "comic" or "escapist" fantasy, such as Manlove sees in the works of many popular fantasists from Morris to Eddison to Cabell. (In his later *The Impulse of Fantasy Literature* [1983], he called these works "anaemic" fantasy.) "Imaginative fantasy" is that which attempts to construct a coherent vision of a transformed reality, and provides the focus of Manlove's chapters on Kingsley, MacDonald, Lewis, Tolkien, and Peake. Nearly all of these authors fail in some crucial way, according to Manlove, who speculates that lack of shared belief between author and audience may make modern fantasy too risky an undertaking, and one that is more often than not doomed to failure. In *The Impulse of Fantasy Literature*, Manlove attempts to identify the reasons people keep writing and reading fantasies despite these pitfalls, and arrives at the conclusion that fantasy is at base a celebration of identity.

Despite their reservations about the genre, Manlove and Irwin did much to establish a set of works to be discussed under the rubric fantasy and a framework for their discussion. Like Rabkin and Todorov, however, these critics tended to focus on the rhetorical and psychological aspects of the genre. Stephen Prickett's 1979 *Victorian Fantasy*, on the other hand, is more purely a historical study, and as such is important in establishing a context for some of the functions of major works in the genre. Far from being self-indulgent escapism, Prickett argues, fantasy narratives provided important means of exploring some of the major concerns of the era—madness, sexuality, childhood, and the hidden worlds revealed by the emerging sciences of biology, chemistry, physiology, and geology. Furthermore, fantasy became a kind of mediator for some of the chief social tensions of the era—progress versus tradition, freedom versus inhibition, prosperity versus poverty, justice versus repression. Although he does not construct a clear taxonomy of fantasy types, his demonstrations of how individual works reacted against and moved beyond the prevailing norms of realism provide an impressive case for the importance of historical research to fantasy scholarship. A

similarly historical work concerning American literature is Brian Attebury's *The Fantasy Tradition in American Literature* (1980), which
sees American fantasists working even more in a kind of "underground,"
given what Attebury finds is a persistent bias against the fantastic in
American folklore and culture. American fantasists, he argues, have
sought to reclaim for the American experience the older storytelling
traditions in the hopes of constructing a uniquely American version of
fairyland.

By the early 1980s, fantasy scholarship was fairly widespread and
reasonably well accepted by the academy. It is even possible to identify
emerging schools of criticism of the genre: While Christine Brooke-
Rose's 1982 *A Rhetoric of the Unreal* draws upon Todorov and later
traditions of European post-structuralist criticism, Ann Swinfen's 1984
In Defence of Fantasy returns clearly to Tolkien as its critical model.
Kathryn Hume's *Fantasy and Mimesis*, also published in 1984, explores
the notion that fantasy may not be a genre at all, but rather a response
to reality opposed to the more traditional mode of mimesis. Roger
Schlobin's 1982 *The Aesthetics of Fantasy Literature and Art*, probably
the first collection of critical essays on the topic, demonstrates a variety
of critical approaches and even conflicting definitions without appearing
to lose its focus, indicating perhaps that the first generation of fantasy
scholarship is at an end.

But future students of fantasy must look beyond academic studies in
order to get a complete picture of how ideas about fantasy have evolved
during the past twenty years. Publishers, fan writers, anthologists, bibliographers, and librarians have all contributed to the establishment not
only of a fantasy canon but also to the terminology and to the establishment of what author Samuel R. Delany calls "reading protocols."
"Adult fantasy," which once was a code word for pornography, became
a kind of critical term largely through the efforts of Lin Carter, who
chose this rubric as the title for a highly successful series of paperback
reprints from Ballantine Books beginning in 1969, and who himself wrote
a popular history of fantasy as part of that series in 1973. Editors Robert
H. Boyer and Kenneth J. Zahorski, in a series of anthologies beginning
in 1977 (and which are widely used in the classroom), did much to popularize such terms as "high fantasy," "low fantasy," and "Christian fantasy." Bibliographies such as those by Roger Schlobin, Diana Waggoner,
and Marshall B. Tymn (in collaboration with Boyer and Zahorski) implicitly add to critical debate not only in their introductions and annota-
tions, but by their very principles of inclusion and classification. The
delineation of such subgenres as "sword and sorcery" and "science fantasy" has been worked out sometimes to incredible detail in the fan press.
And for better or worse, the marketing and acquisitions practices of publishing houses have tended to emphasize certain conventions and narra-

tive modes over others. The multivolume novel or continuing series of novels, for example, have almost become more the norm than the exception, and popular extratextual devices such as maps, genealogies, illustrations, and glossaries have very nearly become forms in themselves. Despite its growing legitimacy, the study of fantasy is far from a settled matter, still very much fragmented by the various communities that have given rise to it, and still uncertain in its critical vocabulary.

THE GROWTH OF SCIENCE FICTION SCHOLARSHIP

If fantasy criticism developed largely as an adjunct to formal literary study, growing from the early isolated defenses of the genre to more theoretical studies and eventually to historical and bibliographical approaches, science fiction criticism evolved in a radically different manner: Its beginnings lay clearly outside the realms of traditional literary discourse, in pulp and fan magazines, and within the specialty presses. It might not be too much of a generalization to say that fantasy scholarship is an outgrowth of English and European critical tradition, while science fiction scholarship, like modern science fiction itself, is largely an American phenomenon: populist, combative, and dominated in its initial stages by the kind of bibliographical and historical concerns that are as much of interest to the collector as to the scholar. In many ways, early science fiction criticism constitutes a unique kind of popular scholarship, and even today the close relationships among author, editor, reader, and critic are an unusual characteristic of science fiction.

From the beginning of the pulp era, letter columns such as "The Eyrie" in *Weird Tales* (founded 1923), "Discussions" in *Amazing Stories* (1926), "The Reader Speaks" in *Wonder Stories* (1929), and "Science Discussions" (later "Brass Tacks") in *Astounding Stories* (1930) debated the merits of stories from previous issues, as well as artwork, editorials, layout, scientific and pseudoscientific matters, and—inevitably—the nature and characteristics of "scientifiction" as a genre (although a term like "genre" would have seemed radically out of place in such columns). It did not take long for correspondence with the magazines and with each other to seem inadequate for some fans, and individually produced "fanzines" began to appear by 1930, with organized fan meeetings and "conventions" only a few years behind. The science fiction folk culture, with its passion for neologisms and grand debates, was under way—and since many of these early fans would in time become professional authors themselves, the vocabulary of fandom gradually would become conflated in part with the vocabulary of the professional author, and in turn with the vocabulary of the publishing industry. Later academic critics, confronted with this makeshift critical tradition which had seemingly grown in virtual isolation from any identifiable literary or critical discourse, found themselves in an almost unprecedented situation, and the relation of fan scholarship to formal scholarship remains a topic of debate within the genre.

What is perhaps the most significant critical work to emerge from the early fan publications concerned itself more with fantasy than with science fiction. H. P. Lovecraft's long essay, *Supernatural Horror in Literature*, was first commissioned for an amateur publication in 1924 and later revised for a fanzine in the 1930s (although the fanzine folded, and the essay finally appeared in the 1939 omnibus volume, *The Outsider and Others*, from Arkham House—which itself began with the devotion of a fan, August Derleth). Lovecraft's work was in part derivative of earlier studies and was as resolutely eccentric as his fiction, but it brought to fandom a tradition of what Lovecraft himself would no doubt have enthusiastically termed "gentlemanly scholarship" and demonstrated that works of academic significance could emerge from the community of pulp magazines and fan writers. Later fan undertakings would range from ambitious histories of the genre to useful but highly specialized concordances (such as a 1968 concordance to the works of E. E. Smith), many of them taking advantage of private collections, correspondence, interviews, and other sources not readily available to later scholars in universities.

After World War II, as science fiction began to move from the exclusive province of magazines into the bookstores and libraries, and as the pulp era died, more thoughtful book reviews and occasional surveys of the field began to appear in the professional magazines as well as in the fan press. In 1947, Lloyd Arthur Eshbach edited for his newly formed Fantasy Press a symposium of articles by well-known science fiction authors *Of Worlds Beyond: The Science of Science Fiction Writing* (probably the first book-length treatment of modern science fiction). The most significant contribution to this symposium, Robert A. Heinlein's "On the Writing of Speculative Fiction," raised important questions about the proper name of the genre (Heinlein preferred "speculative fiction") and about the role of extrapolation (which remains one of the key buzzwords of the field and eventually became the title of an academic journal). Jack Williamson's "The Logic of Fantasy" discussed a number of principles which he saw as governing internal consistency in a fantastic story and which anticipated more formal attempts to describe the genre by later critics. Other essays, by John Taine (Eric Temple Bell), A. E. Van Vogt, L. Sprague de Camp, Edward E. Smith, and John W. Campbell, Jr., focused more narrowly on how to write stories—and indeed, the general thrust of the volume was that of a writers' handbook. Nevertheless, appearing the same year as the Oxford University Press volume which featured essays by Tolkien and Lewis, *Of Worlds Beyond* was in its way as significant to the development of science fiction criticism as the former volume was to the development of fantasy criticism.

Formal academic attention to science fiction is also generally said to have begun in 1947, with the publication of J. O. Bailey's historical study *Pilgrims through Space and Time: Trends and Patterns in Scientific and Utopian Fiction*. Written mostly during the 1930s and published not by a university press but by a New York bookseller, Bailey's work is in two parts: a historical survey that outlines the prehistory of the genres, focuses heavily on the period 1870–1915, and appends a chapter written later on post–1915 science fiction; and an attempt at identifying various narrative characteristics and themes of the genre. Although the book's rather mechanical taxonomizing of concepts provides little in the way of a coherent critical approach, and although some members of the fan community objected to the short shrift given magazine science fiction, Bailey's work did much to establish the groundwork for all future historical studies of the genre. Together with Everett Bleiler's lengthy bibliography, *The Checklist of Fantastic Literature*, which appeared the following year (also from a specialty press), it also helped establish a canon of early works, provided evidence of a long and significant tradition of science fiction writing, and developed a context for discussion of emerging trends and themes.

Bailey's study might have had greater impact at the time had it not come up against the distrust of some fans who viewed him as an "outsider." "Inside" and "outside" had by the 1940s already become significant categories to readers of science fiction when discussing critical treatments of the genre; perhaps sensitive to a scathing 1939 essay in *Harper's* in which mainstream critic Bernard DeVoto attacked the pulps, readers had become wary of any such attention tendered by "academics" or "literary types" (especially if they were not American: William L. Hamling devoted an entire editorial in a 1953 issue of the science fiction magazine *Imagination* to a sneering attack on an early essay about science fiction by the Polish writer Stanislaw Lem).[21] At the same time, writers and editors within the genre seemed anxious to capitalize on such "outside" attention, and *The Magazine of Fantasy and Science Fiction* did not hesitate throughout the 1950s to parade on its back cover endorsements from Clifton Fadiman, Orville Prescott, Basil Davenport, and other "literary types." Davenport himself wrote a short study of science fiction in 1955, *Inquiry into Science Fiction*, in which he discussed with some sophistication questions of definition, the distinction between science fiction and fantasy, and such subgenres as space opera, "scientific science fiction," and speculative science fiction.

A literary essay by a mainstream figure that was in many ways quite similar to Davenport's was Kingsley Amis' *New Maps of Hell* (1960), based on a series of lectures given at the Christian Gauss seminars at Princeton. Again raising questions of definition and the relationship to fantasy, Amis begins with a breezy survey of the early history of the genre and settles in to base his defense of it largely on the satirical and anti-utopian works that emerged from *Galaxy* magazine in the 1950s, and in particular on works by Ray Bradbury, Robert Sheckley, and Frederik Pohl (whom Amis characterizes as "the most consistently able writer science fiction, in the modern sense, has yet produced").[22] By focusing on science fiction largely as a satirical mode, Amis was able to link the modern genre directly with a respectable literary tradition; by focusing on contemproary works, he was able to draw attention to science fiction as a vital ongoing phenomenon and not as a curiosity of literary history or popular culture. For these reasons (as well as Amis' reputation), *New Maps of Hell* probably had greater impact outside the genre than any earlier critical work—and its influence within the genre was assured by its being reprinted by Ballantine Books in its mass-market series of science fiction paperbacks.

Meanwhile, "inside" criticism and theory continued its own development in books as well as magazines. Following Eshbach's lead, Reginald Bretnor edited three collections of original essays on science fiction in 1953, 1974, and 1976. The first of these, *Modern Science Fiction: Its Meaning and Its Future*, was a comprehensive attempt to assess the status of the genre in 1953, with contributions from John W. Campbell, Jr., Anthony Boucher, Isaac Asimov, Arthur C. Clarke, Philip Wylie, Fletcher Pratt, L. Sprague de Camp, and others. The collection introduced a number of definitions of the genre and raised a number of issues—including relationships to the mainstream, "social science fiction," religious themes, and the influence of publishers—which would remain key topics for discussion in later scholarship. Bretnor's second collection, *Science Fiction Today and Tomorrow*, reassessed the field from the vantage point of 1974 and featured essays by Pohl, Frank Herbert, Theodore Sturgeon, James Gunn, Gordon R. Dickson, Jack Williamson, Poul Anderson, and a number of other writers. While some of these essays covered the same ground as the earlier collection, others focused more on the growing acceptance of science fiction as literature (and the concomitant need for critical methods and vocabularies), while others focused more on technique. Bretnor's third collection, *The Craft of Science Fiction*, emphasized technique in particular, although several of the essays contained valuable critical and historical insights.

L. Sprague de Camp's *Science Fiction Handbook* appeared in 1953, and the anonymously edited collection (with an introduction by Basil Davenport) *The Science Fiction Novel: Imagination and Social Criticism*, based on talks by major writers at the University of Chicago, in 1959. While de Camp's book (revised and reissued in 1975) is very much a how-to manual, the Davenport collection of essays by Heinlein, C. M. Kornbluth, Alfred Bester, and Robert Bloch was one of the first to raise significant questions regarding what might be called the "social con-science" (or lack of it) in the genre. Kornbluth's essay in particular comments on the failure of the genre to fully realize its potential, and this attitude of critical self-examination is evident in the other essays as well. Although a slim volume, this collection is representative of a ma-turing of the genre's self-awareness that was also reflected in the mag-azine criticism of Damon Knight and James Blish.

Magazine criticism, in fact, was perhaps even more important in es-tablishing a common set of critical assumptions than the various books we have been discussing. Blish published a four-part survey of "The Science in Science Fiction" in 1951 and 1952 issues of *Science Fiction Quarterly*, and James Gunn published several articles (derived from his master's thesis) on "The Philosophy of Science Fiction" and "The Plot-forms of Science Fiction" in *Dynamic Science Fiction* in 1953 and 1954. Such essays drew both on the authors' academic training and on their fa-miliarity with the genre as readers and authors, and thus represent the earliest attempts at deriving a consensus critical vocabulary for the genre.

Blish, with his critical assessments of magazine fiction (collected under the name "William Atheling, Jr.," in *The Issue at Hand* [1964] and *More Issues at Hand* [1970]), and Knight, with his reviews published in the professional magazines (collected as *In Search of Wonder* [1967]), each held the genre to rigorous standards of critical analysis during the crucial years of the early 1950s, identifying major themes and concepts with a clarity that would prove of great value to later scholars seeking an understanding of this period. The importance of the genre's major in-ternal critics in establishing a context for later science fiction and fantasy criticism cannot be overestimated, although it is sometimes surprising how few academic researchers are familiar with the work of these critics/reviewers. From the synoptic early reviews of the pulps and early digest magazines (sometimes with several books neatly disposed of in a simple paragraph or even on a chart), genre reviewing has emerged as a sig-nificant body of critical work in its own right, with Algis Budrys (who has also contributed to academic publications) the most notable example since 1965. Budrys's reviews in *Galaxy* (collected in *Benchmarks: Galaxy Bookshelf*, 1985) and later *The Magazine of Fantasy and Science Fiction* often digress into critical theory and inevitably seek to establish a context for the book under discussion, and his essay "Paradise Charted" (pub-lished in *Triquarterly*, Fall 1980) remains the most useful and insightful short survey of the development of modern science fiction.

Despite the presence of such acute critics as Blish, Knight, and Bud-rys, the magazines did not entirely forgo the celebratory and often defensive traditions of earlier fan criticism. Sam Moskowitz's sketches of major writers in the genre, originally published in magazines and gathered into two volumes in 1963 (*Explorers of the Infinite*) and 1966 (*Seekers of Tomorrow*), tended distinctly toward uncritical celebration and dogged source-hunting, sometimes sacrificing accuracy of detail for the dramatic anecdote. Yet these volumes were widely read and were for a considerable time virtually the only published source of biographical data about a number of writers. More important than these volumes, as works of scholarship, are Moskowitz's various historical anthologies of early science fiction which began appearing in the late 1960s.

Yet there was still little dialogue between "insiders" and "outsiders," and with the exception of Bailey, few of the "outsiders" were professional scholars formally engaging the genre in any systematic way. The so-called academic awakening, associated with the study of science fiction and fantasy in universities, would not really get under way until the 1970s, and it came about not only because of literary scholars turning their attention to science fiction, but because of science fiction writers such as James Gunn, Jack Williamson, Brian Aldiss, and Samuel R. Delany entering the arena of literary scholarship.

Probably the first academic study of science fiction to be published under the imprimatur of a university press was Robert M. Philmus' *Into the Unknown: The Evolution of Science Fiction from Francis Godwin to H. G. Wells*, published by the University of California Press in 1970. Oxford University Press had published H. Bruce Franklin's anthology *Future Perfect: American Science Fiction of the Nineteenth Century*, with its extensive critical commentary, in 1966, but Philmus' book was exclusively a critical and historical study, more carefully researched and theoretically coherent than similar material covered in Bailey's 1947 volume. Somewhat dated in the light of later research, it remains a pioneer study.

During the 1970s, academic studies of science fiction began to appear with increasing regularity. Bowling Green University Popular Press issued Thomas D. Clareson's *SF: The Other Side of Realism*, a collection of essays by various hands, in 1971; and Clareson's *Science Fiction Criticism: An Annotated Checklist* appeared from Kent State University Press in 1972, the first extensive bibliography of writings about science fiction. Clareson, a fan-turned-academic who had been involved in the first Modern Language Association seminars on science fiction and who founded the journal *Extrapolation*, continued to edit volumes of essays throughout the 1970s, and contributed much valuable research of his own concerning the early history of American science fiction and the lost-race narrative in particular, culminating in *Some Kind of Paradise: The Emergence of American Science Fiction* (Greenwood Press, 1985).

David Ketterer's *New Worlds for Old: The Apocalyptic Imagination*,

Science Fiction, and American Literature (1974) was one of the first theoretically rigorous attempts to locate science fiction in a tradition of literary discourse (what Ketterer called the "apocalyptic"); and in 1975 David Samuelson's *Visions of Tomorrow* provided detailed readings of six classic science fiction novels, demonstrating convincingly that the best science fiction could stand up to the kind of sophisticated textual and thematic analysis traditionally associated with the realistic novel. That same year saw the appearance of a slim volume by Robert Scholes, a renowned critic whose interest in narrative had brought him increasingly closer to the genre over a number of years. *Structural Fabulation*, based on a series of lectures delivered at Notre Dame, contained some broad theoretical proclamations and limited analysis of individual works, but it did demonstrate that science fiction was beginning to draw the attention of the critical "establishment," much in the same way that Kingsley Amis' 1960 volume seemed to represent the attention of the literary mainstream.

By the late 1970s, enough of a body of criticism had been established that it no longer seemed necessary for each new volume to be comprehensively theoretical or historical in scope. Paul A. Carter's *The Creation of Tomorrow* (1977) focused exclusively on the history of American magazine science fiction, while Walter Meyers' *Aliens and Linguists* (1980) dealt with language in science fiction, Patricia Warrick's *The Cybernetic Imagination in Science Fiction* (1980) dealt with artificial intelligence, Warren Wagar's *Terminal Visions* (1982) dealt with eschatological themes, and Casey Fredericks' *The Future of Eternity* dealt with mythologies and myth systems. Theoretical models for the discussion of the genre were presented by Darko Suvin (*Metamorphoses of Science Fiction* [1979]), Gary K. Wolfe (*The Known and the Unknown: The Iconography of Science Fiction* [1979]), and Mark Rose (*Alien Encounters* [1981]).

Of these theoretical studies, the most widely discussed and debated has undoubtedly been Suvin's. Defining the essential quality of science fiction as "cognitive estrangement," Suvin provides a carefully reasoned argument for setting the genre apart from related genres of fantastic literature and for treating utopian fiction as a subgenre. He is careful to place science fiction in the context of an intellectual tradition of sociopolitical thought and, in the second half of his volume, analyzes this tradition in terms of the early history of the genre both in Europe and in America. His work is significant not only for bringing to science fiction the methods of structuralist and Marxist literary analysis (and for bringing science fiction to the attention of these disciplines), but also for the attention it pays to Eastern European science fiction and the utopian tradition. While a number of readers have complained of Suvin's rather dense style, the rigor of his methodology helped to set new standards for the discussion of science fiction in the context of intellectual history.

An equally rigorous and challenging critic emerged during this time from within the genre itself. Samuel R. Delany's critical writings, collected in *The Jewel-Hinged Jaw* (1977), *The American Shore* (1978), and *Starboard Wine* (1984), focus largely on the kinds of language that make up fantastic narratives and the evolution of conventional ways of reading, or "protocols," that enable the reader to relate such language meaningfully to experience. Delany's frequently brilliant, often pyrotechnic critical approach draws equally on the highly personal experiences of a young fan turned author and on extensive study of European post-structuralist modes of analysis. More than any other critic, Delany has shown promise of bridging the gap between the traditions of the science fiction writer-critic and the academic, but largely because of this his essays have not always been as widely or well received as they deserve. (Part of the problem, too, is their relative inaccessibility from having been published in hardbound editions by a specialty press.)

If "academic" critics began to focus largely on science fiction in a broader intellectual context, a number of writers in the genre began to turn to its own internal history and development, and the 1970s saw a number of ambitious histories of the genre, followed soon by more detailed and personal memoirs and autobiographies. The first and best of the histories was Brian Aldiss' *Billion Year Spree: The True History of Science Fiction* (1973), which immediately generated controversy by its assertion that science fiction is a Romantic, post-Gothic narrative mode which began with Mary Shelley's *Frankenstein* in 1817. Using that novel as his starting point, Aldiss proceeds to persuasively demonstrate how the fundamental concerns laid out by Shelley—the Faustian theme, the dual nature of human consciousness, the use and misuse of science—have informed science fiction works throughout the nineteenth and twentieth centuries. Aldiss' British perspective provides him not only with an acute sensitivity to the traditions of the English novel that science fiction initially worked within and against, but also with a certain distance from the American magazine tradition, which he treats with a rare objectivity and good humor.

Much closer to the "official" American history (in the sense of one which conforms to the most widely held beliefs of many writers and fans) is James Gunn's lavishly illustrated *Alternate Worlds: The Illustrated History of Science Fiction* (1975). Gunn's work is avowedly a popular history rather than a work of detailed scholarship, and it is valuable particularly for its treatment of the evolution of science fiction in terms of the growth of technology and the evolution of techniques of mass market publishing. Gunn makes few controversial claims regarding the major figures in the field, but he does provide the perspective of a working writer, and he conveys a sense of science fiction as a profession and a popular art form in a way that more purely literary treatments of the genre often miss. A similar "writer's" perspective may be found in Lester del Rey's resolutely idiosyncratic *The World of Science Fiction: the History of a Subculture* (1979), a highly anecdotal and opinionated survey that covers much of the same ground as Gunn, but with more attention paid to the fan subculture and to del Rey's own career.

Where there are histories, there will be bibliographies and reference works. Everett F. Bleiler's *Checklist of Fantastic Literature* (1948) long served as the standard bibliography of the genre, but with the rise of more specialized audiences for bibliographies—libraries, teachers, and scholars as well as collectors—there came a need for more detailed and selective bibliographies and encyclopedias. For a genre still in the process of establishing its basic canon and lineage, this came both as a blessing and a curse: Authors found themselves entombed before their times, reputations were concretized in a few glib paragraphs, obscure authors were elevated to permanence, and younger authors were often relegated to limbo. More than in most fields of literary study, the reference work in science fiction (or fantasy) is inevitably a critical act. Early and fairly comprehensive bibliographies such as R. Reginald's *Stella Nova* (1970) (expanded in 1979 to the massive two-volume *Science Fiction and Fantasy Literature*) were relatively uncontroversial, but the collaborative efforts that led to Neil Barron's attempt at a definitive science fiction bibliography for libraries and scholars with *Anatomy of Wonder* (1976; second edition, 1981) seemed to constitute a consensus critical assessment of the genre. Particularly in its second edition, Barron's bibliography is invaluable, as is Peter Nicholls' *The Science Fiction Encyclopedia* (1979). Much of the value of these books is that they do offer critical judgments, but some critics have argued, for example, that the Nicholls volume seems biased toward the "New Wave" or that the Barron volume (in its first edition) slighted non-English-language science fiction.

While the Nicholls and Barron volumes were compiled by teams of scholars working together, other reference works have solicited contributions from wide ranges of authors and academics, with the result that they often partake both of the essay collection and the encyclopedic dictionary. Curtis C. Smith's *Twentieth Century Science Fiction Writers* (1981) is among the most complete of such volumes, with entries on over 600 authors consisting of short essays by various critics and bibliographies compiled sometimes by the editor. David Cowart and Thomas L. Wymer's *Twentieth Century American Science Fiction Writers* (1981), a volume in Gale Research's *Dictionary of Literary Biography*, follows a similar format but attempts to focus the essays somewhat by the rubric "literary biography"; this volume ran into some problems with its sometimes arbitrary assignment of author and critic-essayist, although in general its essays are more detailed than those in the Smith volume. But by far the most ambitious undertaking of this sort was the Salem Press *Survey of Science Fiction Literature* (1979), edited nominally by Frank Magill but with most of the work done by Keith Neilson. Focusing on 500 key works of science fiction, this five-volume set features original essays on these works by an army of scholars and critics. Apart from the critical compromises implicit in selecting works for inclusion, these essays are inevitably uneven and widely divergent in their critical approaches. Nevertheless, the volume represents one of the most exhaustive critical undertakings ever devoted to a popular genre.

As a result of all these reference works and essay collections, for a while more critics were spending time writing general-purpose assessments of authors than were contributing to the major journals in the field. *Extrapolation*, the first academic journal on science fiction, had existed since 1959, growing from a semiannual newsletter for the Modern Language Association's Seminar on Science Fiction to a full-fledged journal. Under the editorship of Thomas Clareson from its founding until 1986, it remains the most eclectic of the field's journals, and it was for years the source of the standard annual bibliography of scholarship until these bibliographies began to be issued separately by Kent State University Press, which now publishes the journal as well. (In 1985, the annual bibliography returned to *Extrapolation*.) *Foundation*, the first British science fiction journal, appeared in 1972 and consistently features essays of the greatest clarity of style; many of the contributors are the scholars who worked on Nicholls' *Encyclopedia*. Like that work, *Foundation* partakes of certain traditions of fan scholarship and has perhaps won greater acceptance among fans and writers than the other journals. *Science-Fiction Studies* (*SFS*) was founded in 1973 under the editorship of Darko Suvin and R. D. Mullen and soon became associated with political, sociological, and semiotic approaches to the genre, and with discussions of non-English-language science fiction. By far the most theoretical of the periodicals, *SFS* has also had the most consistent viewpoint, despite its own protestations of eclecticism.

By the mid–1970s, these three journals were publishing a combined total of nine issues per year, and at least a half-dozen university presses were including science fiction and fantasy scholarship on their lists. At least five of these—Oxford, Indiana, Southern Illinois, Kent State, and Bowling Green—would commit to publishing series of studies on fantastic literature. Specialty presses as well, most notably Borgo and Starmont House, began issuing series of individual author studies, critical and reference works, and collections of interviews. G. K. Hall began issuing a series of library-bound bibliographies of individual science fiction and fantasy authors, and Greenwood Press undertook an extensive series of original studies and collections of essays under the editorship of Marshall Tymn as "Contributions to the Study of Science Fiction and Fantasy." In 1984, UMI Research Press began to mine unconverted doctoral dissertations for a series of "Studies in Speculative Fiction." Taplinger and Ungar issued series of essay collections. Textbook publishers, too, found a market for science fiction anthologies and texts, as did library reprint houses and yet more reference book publishers.

Whether this relatively sudden blossoming of essays and books about science fiction and fantasy meets a genuine need is of course questionable, and raises again the question discussed earlier concerning the potential academic exploitation of the field. At the same time, it is apparent that interest in the fantastic is generally far greater than it once was, and that it cannot be accounted for solely by library markets for new books or by ambitious college faculty. Those who have contributed to the recent spate of reference books and critical anthologies include not only academics, but fans who had previously published in unpaid fanzines, professional authors from within the genre, and "literary essayists" whose interest in the work is neither purely professional nor purely academic. The problem is that each of these groups brings to their work a different set of critical assumptions and terminology, and the resulting confusion arguably compromised the coherence of a great many of the critical volumes on the genre that have appeared in the last decade or so. While it might reasonably be argued that science fiction scholarship is no more eclectic in its terminology than literary scholarship in general, it is also true that there has been too little attention paid to the etiology and etymology of some of the more specialized terms, and perhaps a concomitant failure in communication among the various communities that have contributed to and continue to contribute to the scholarship of fantastic literature. Scholars and fans almost certainly need to pay more attention to the best of each other's work, and there may even be insights from such work that the "pro" community of writers, editors, and publishers could find useful. It may seem a simplistic claim, but only when these various communities begin to look at each other's words can they fairly evaluate each other's ideas.

NOTES

1. Algis Budrys, "Books," *Magazine of Fantasy and Science Fiction* 64, no. 1 (January 1983); 19. Budrys was reviewing George Slusser, Eric S. Rabkin, and Robert Scholes' *Bridges to Fantasy* (Carbondale: Southern Illinois University Press, 1982). Rabkin's response to the review appeared in *Fantasy Newsletter*, no. 60 (June/July 1983). The earlier attacks on academia include Lloyd Biggle, Jr., "Science Fiction Goes to College: Groves and Morasses of Academe," *Riverside Quarterly* 6 (April 1974); 100–109, and "The Morasses of Academe Revisited," *Analog* 98 (September 1978): 146–163; William Tenn, "Jazz Then, Musicology Now," *The Magazine of Fantasy and Science Fiction* 42 (May 1972): 107–110; Ben Bova, "Teaching Science Fiction," *Analog* 93 (June 1974): 5–8; and Lester del Rey, "The Siren Song of Academe," *Galaxy* 36 (March 1975): 69–80, reprinted in *Antaeus* 25/26 (Spring/Summer 1977); 312–322. Russell Letson's essay "Contributions to the Critical Dialogue: As an Academic Sees It," delivered at the 1986 International Conference on the Fantastic in the Arts but unpublished at the time of this writing, is perhaps the most intelligent discussion of this debate so far.

2. Everett F. Bleiler, "Pilgrim Award Acceptance Address," *SFRA Newsletter*, no. 123 (July/August 1984): 12.

3. R. D. Mullen, "Every Critic His Own Aristotle," *Science-Fiction Studies*, no. 10 (November 1976): 311. The book under review was Eric S. Rabkin's *The Fantastic in Literature* (Princeton: Princeton University Press, 1976).

4. Joseph Addison, *The Spectator* 411 (June 21, 1712).

5. Quoted in Lilian R. Furst, *Romanticism in Perspective* (New York: Humanities Press, 1970), p. 332.

6. Cited in "Imagination," *Oxford English Dictionary*.

7. William Blake, "A Vision of the Last Judgment," in Geoffrey Keynes, ed., *Complete Writings* (London: Oxford University Press, 1967), p. 604.

8. Samuel Taylor Coleridge, *Biographia Literaria*, excerpted in *Selected Poetry and Prose*, ed. Donald R. Stauffer (New York: Modern Library, 1951), p. 156.

9. Coleridge, p. 263.

10. Stephen Prickett, *Victorian Fantasy* (Bloomington: Indiana University Press, 1979), p. 2.

11. Ruth Amelia Berman, "Suspending Disbelief: The Development of Fantasy as a Literary Genre in Nineteenth-Century British Fiction as Represented by Four Leading Periodicals: *Edinburgh Review*, *Blackwood's*, *Fraser's*, and *Cornhill*," Ph.D. diss., University of Minnesota, 1979.

12. Quoted in Donald P. Haase, "Romantic Theory of the Fantastic," in Frank N. Magill, ed., *Survey of Modern Fantasy Literature* (Englewood Cliffs, N.J.: Salem Press, 1983), vol. 5, p. 2251.

13. Quoted in Gary K. Wolfe, "Contemporary Theories of the Fantastic," in Magill, V, p. 2221.

14. *Adam Bede* (New York: Signet, 1961 [1859]), p. 176.

15. Terry Eagleton, *Literary Theory: An Introduction* (Minneapolis: University of Minnesota Press, 1983), p. 27.

16. Quoted in Wolfe, p. 2222.

17. Quoted in Wolfe, p. 2222.

18. J. R. R. Tolkien, "On Fairy-Stories," *A Tolkien Reader* (New York: Ballantine, 1966), p. 26.

19. Eric S. Rabkin, *The Fantastic in Literature* (Princeton: Princeton University Press, 1976), p. 227.

20. W. R. Irwin, *The Game of the Impossible* (Urbana: University of Illinois Press, 1976), p. 4.

21. The DeVoto essay was titled "Doom beyond Jupiter," *Harper's* 179 (September 1939); 445–448; a more sympathetic treatment of the genre by Clemence Dane ("American Fairy Tales," *North American Review* 242 [September 1936]; 143–152) was generally overlooked. Hamling's editorial (*Imagination; Stories of Science and Fantasy* 4, no. 4 [May 1953]; 4–5) was largely an anticommunist diatribe that attempted to argue that, since science fiction was written for entertainment and money, it was proof of the advantages of American freedom.

22. Kingsley Amis, *New Maps of Hell* (New York: Ballantine, 1960), p. 102.

CRITICAL TERMS FOR SCIENCE FICTION AND FANTASY

Cross-references to other entries in the glossary are marked with an asterisk (*), except for the terms "science fiction," "fantasy," and "genre" (which appear too frequently to make this practical). References to enumerated sources in the list of Works Consulted are given in brackets, while citations to works not listed there are given in context in the entry itself. In a few cases, in which a term is so widespread or so variant in usages that citations would prove impractical, no source is given.

A

ABSURD. Albert Camus' term for the human condition (*Le Mythe de Sisyphe*, 1942; trans. "The Myth of Sisyphus," 1955), which became commonplace in criticism after Martin Esslin used it in 1961 to describe a group of postwar dramatists—Beckett, Ionesco, Pinter, and others—who rejected representational techniques of the realistic theatre in favor of a variety of fantasy devices [44]. Since then, the term has been applied to fiction as well, in particular the fiction of those authors like Beckett who are associated with the Theatre of the Absurd. Many, if not most, absurd works are in some degree fantasies, and some partake of the thematic furniture of science fiction as well. For example, Eugene Ionesco's *Rhinoceros* (1960) concerns the transformation of humans into beasts, while Samuel Beckett's *Endgame* (1957) is set in a desolate world resembling that of Post-Holocaust* fiction [198]. Peter Nicholls has also described an "absurdist" tradition within science fiction, which includes works of J. G. Ballard, Kurt Vonnegut, Jr., Harlan Ellison, Brian Aldiss, and Thomas M. Disch [144]. Finally, the term is often applied to works of fantasy that prefigure the term itself, such as those of Franz Kafka, Raymond Roussel, or Alfred Jarry.

ACADEMIC. Used both as an adjective and a noun to describe the involvement of professional scholars and teachers in the criticism, history, theory, and teaching of science fiction. Such a meaning might seem obvious, but the term has gained a great many overtones, usually either disparaging or defensive, and has come rather imprecisely to be contrasted both with fan or amateur scholarship in the field, and with the various "internal" works of history and criticism generated by science fiction and fantasy writers themselves. In this usage, the "academic" is often regarded as an outsider trained in traditional humanistic methodologies that are sometimes felt to be inadequate for science fiction; interestingly, the term is seldom applied to university scientists or even social scientists, suggesting that it refers not necessarily to the academic world per se, but specifically to inhabitants of English or history departments in universities.

ADAPTATION. E. M. Forster's term for fantasy narratives that recast already familiar materials; for example, C. S. Lewis' *Till We Have Faces* (1956) is an adaptation of the Cupid and Psyche myth [87]. Later, the term came to be used more broadly and popularly to refer to the recasting of story materials from one medium into another; the film *Charly* (1968), for example, is an adaptation of Daniel Keyes' novel *Flowers for Algernon* (1966), while Alan Dean Foster's novel *Alien* (1979) conversely is an adaptation of the Ridley Scott film of that name. (See also Novelization*.) In the latter sense, the term has become somewhat problematical as "package" contracts and "property development" specialists help to create confusion regarding the extent to which books and films are in fact created separately. A projected film production may have such financial impact on a book contract that film considerations become part of the conception of the novel itself.

ADDITIVE WORLD. (alternatively, "augmented world"). A fictional world which is "notably fuller, richer, and more varied and vivid than our everyday reality," according to Kathryn Hume [102]. Hume sees this, along with Subtractive Worlds* and Contrastive Worlds,* as one of three principal ways a fictional world can comment on reality.

ADULT FANTASY. Term popularized by Lin Carter of Ballantine Books for a series of fantasy reprints and original anthologies that Carter began editing in 1969 [47]. Probably based more on marketing considerations than generic characteristics, the term has come to refer to any fantasy narrative not specifically directed toward a juvenile audience. In an entirely different sphere of popular culture, the term sometimes refers to pornography.

ADVENTURE DOMINANT. American science fiction from 1926 to 1938, according to a chronology suggested by Isaac Asimov in 1962; the period from 1938 to 1950 he labeled "technology dominant," and from 1950 to the time he was writing as "sociology dominant" [14]. Later, with Asimov's concurrence, James Gunn suggested a fourth period, "style dominant," which began in the mid–1960s, presumably under the influence of the New Wave* [97]. Earlier, writing in 1953, Asimov had used the term "adventure science fiction," which was intended to distinguish the second of four eras in the history of science fiction (the

others being the "primitive era," from 1815 to 1926; the Campbell Era,*
from 1938 to 1945—which Gunn later labeled "science-dominant"—and
the "atomic era" of post–1945 science fiction, dominated by Social Science
Fiction* as represented in the pages of *Galaxy* magazine, founded in
1950 [35].

ADVENTURE SCIENCE FICTION. See ADVENTURE DOMINANT.

ALL-AGES FANTASY. A rather unsatisfactory term used by some critics
and bibliographers to refer to fantasy novels that appeal both to children
and adults [199].

ALLEGORY. "A wall decoration with a label attached," according to
David Lindsay (*Devil's Tor*, 1932). Allegory in its usual sense of
symbolizing the immaterial through fixed fictional figures has been
disclaimed by a number of other fantasy writers as well, most notably
C. S. Lewis, who in *The Allegory of Love* (1936), a critical study of
medieval allegory, contrasted allegory with the Sacramentalism* or
Symbolism* that came to characterize his own fantasy writing [119].
Some of this resistance to allegory is almost certainly a reaction to
persistent attempts among critics and reviewers to read fantasies as
allegories. Authors from George MacDonald to J. R. R. Tolkien have
complained of such reviews. (In Tolkien's case, for example, one
commentator viewed *The Lord of the Rings* as an allegory of World
War II.) Nevertheless, the early history of fantastic literature is closely
allied with allegory in works such as Edmund Spenser's *Faerie Queene*
(1596) or Jonathan Swift's *Gulliver's Travels* (1726), and the allegorical
tradition has not altogether died out in modern fantastic writing, as
evidenced by works such as George Orwell's *Animal Farm* (1945) or
William Golding's *Lord of the Flies* (1954).

ALLOPLASTIC. The anthropologist Géza Róheim suggested that one
distinction between primitive and technological societies is the means
by which they seek integration with the environment: Primitive societies
tend to "autoplastic" means, manipulating the body to suit the perceived
environment (as in surgical rites of passage), while technological societies
use "alloplastic" means, manipulating the environment to make it more
hospitable (*Australian Totemism*, 1925). Gary K. Wolfe has applied this
distinction to science fiction, noting in particular how the alloplastic
fantasy expresses itself through such concepts as "terraforming" or the
autoplastic in such stories as Robert A. Heinlein's "Waldo" [182].

ALTERITY. The quality or state of "otherness"; sometimes used to describe the reversal of Ground Rules* or Displacement* characteristic of fantastic narratives [106].

ALTERNATE HISTORY. A narrative premise claimed equally by science fiction and fantasy—namely, that time contains infinite branches and that universes may exist in which, for example, the Allies lost World War II (Philip K. Dick's *The Man in the High Castle*, 1962) or the Spanish Armada was victorious (Phyllis Eisenstein's *Shadow of Earth*, 1979, or Keith Roberts' *Pavane*, 1962). One of the earliest genre treatments of this theme, Murray Leinster's "Sidewise in Time" (1934), is clearly intended as science fiction. The theme has been present in the genre at least since 1926, although Darko Suvin has identified a number of "alternate histories" published as early as 1871. Suvin's definition, somewhat broader than the commonly accepted use of the term, relates the alternative history to utopian or satirical fiction, identifying it as "that form of SF in which an alternative locus (in space, time, etc.) that shares the material and causal verisimilitude of the writer's world is used to articulate different possible solutions of societal problems, those problems being of sufficient importance to require an alteration in the overall history of the narrated world" [188]. Another bibliography of such works, by Barton C. Hacker and Gordon B. Chamberlain, appeared in *Extrapolation* 22, no. 4 (Winter 1981).

ALTERNATE WORLD. See ALTERNATE HISTORY. The term is also occasionally applied, as in James Gunn's history of the genre, to any of the imagined worlds of science fiction or fantasy [97].

ANACHRONISM. An object, character, event, custom, or language pattern chronologically inappropriate to its setting. Usually regarded as one of the hazards of writing any fiction with a historical setting and the bane of inexperienced or careless authors, anachronism has, however, been cited by L. Sprague de Camp as one of the principal techniques employed in humorous or comic science fiction; the technique is used to good effect, for example, in Mark Twain's *A Connecticut Yankee in King Arthur's Court* (1889) [84].

ANAEMIC FANTASY. C. N. Manlove's characterization of a number of fantasy authors whom he sees as yielding to self-indulgence and self-consciousness in their narratives and avoiding "the harsh facts of pain, loss, ugliness and evil." Among authors he includes in this category are William Morris, Lord Dunsany, E. R. Eddison, and Peter Beagle [131].

ANALOGY. The rhetorical device of comparison of the familiar with the unfamiliar, identified by Darko Suvin as an essential Protocol* for reading science fiction; any "significant SF text," he argues, is "always to be read as an analogy." [187].

ANATOMY. Northrop Frye's term for Menippean* or Varronian satire— a prose fiction work that is heavily expository and covers a wide range of subject matter, such as Robert Burton's *Anatomy of Melancholy* (1621). According to Frye, the genre includes Utopian* works as well as works of fantasy such as Charles Kingsley's *The Water Babies* (1863) [92].

ANIMAL FANTASY. Any narratives focusing on self-conscious animals or communities of animals. Of broader scope than Beast-Fables,* such fantasies are usually not set in a Secondary World,* but rather posit hidden or unknown aspects of animal behavior. According to Ann Swinfen, such tales draw on the traditions of folklore, animal fables, animal satires, naturalists' tales, and the use of animal characters in fantasy in general [189].

ANIMISM. The attribution of spiritual motives to natural phenomena. Animism probably entered fantasy from early religion by way of folklore; at any rate, this convention has become a staple even of nonreligious fantasy.

ANTHOLOGY. "A gathering of flowers," literally, and used in fantastic literature as elsewhere to denote a collection of writings by diverse hands (as opposed to "collections" of stories by a single author). In science fiction especially, however, the anthology gained considerable historical significance during the 1940s and 1950s as a means of defining the genre and establishing its major texts and trends; since then, the anthology has continued to exert far greater influence than in most other popular genres. One might even argue that, with its various subtypes, the anthology has itself become a subgenre of science fiction, with its own aesthetic and critical principles.

Donald A. Wollheim's *The Pocket Book of Science Fiction* (1943) is often credited as the first true genre anthology, although earlier books edited by Phil Stong and others had drawn some material from the science fiction and fantasy Pulps.* But it was Raymond J. Healy and J. Francis McComas' *Adventures in Time and Space* (1946) that is generally viewed as having outlined the parameters of the modern genre, particularly as developed in John W. Campbell, Jr.'s *Astounding Science Fiction.* That same year, some months earlier, saw Groff Conklin's *The Best of Science Fiction,* which with its thematic organization into six categories presaged the "theme" anthologies (such as *Invaders of Earth*, 1952) for which Conklin would become famous. In addition to theme anthologies, other types that have remained popular are "original" anthologies—made up of stories not previously published and pioneered by Raymond J. Healy's *New Tales of Space and Time* (1951) and Frederik Pohl's *Star* series for Ballantine Books (which in turn led to later anthology series by E. J. Carnell, Damon Knight, Terry Carr, Robert Silverberg, and others, to the point where such anthologies rivaled the magazines in periodicity); the "best of the year" anthology, begun by E. F. Bleiler and T. E. Dikty with *The Best Science Fiction Stories 1949* and most famously practiced by Judith Merril from 1956 to 1968; the individual magazine anthologies, such as John W. Campbell, Jr.'s *The Astounding Science Fiction Anthology* (1952), Samuel Mines' *Best from Startling Stories* (1953), and numerous later series from *Galaxy, Astounding/ Analog*, and *The Magazine of Fantasy and Science Fiction*; the award anthologies, including the three volumes of *The Hugo Winners*, edited by Isaac Asimov from 1962 to 1977, and the annual *Nebula Award Stories* by various editors from 1966 to the present; and text anthologies, designed for classroom use, such as James Gunn's four-volume *The Road to Science Fiction* (1977–1982).

ANTICIPATION. Identified by Darko Suvin as a subgenre of science fiction which includes tales "located in the historical future of the author's society," as opposed to Extrapolation,* which often exaggerates one or more specific features of the author's society or depends upon technological advances that may alter that society radically. Suvin cites no specific examples, but H. G. Wells' "A Story of Days to Come" might be a likely candidate [187].

ANTICIPATORY ILLUSION. (German, *Vor-Schein*). Marxist philosopher Ernst Bloch's term (*Asthetic des Vor-Scheins*, 1974) to describe how fairy tales can mirror social processes by providing settings in which reason may be used to realize the desires of fantasy [217].

ANTI-EXPECTED. A narrative event that signals a reversal of Ground Rules* in that it is unexpected in the sense of being thought impossible. According to Eric S. Rabkin, this signals the fantastic in a way that the merely unexpected or the Dis-expected* does not [156].

ANTI-FANTASY. Tales that capture the reader's emotions rather than his intellect, or that compromise the cognitive acceptance of the fantastic through appeal to logical plausibility or archaic beliefs, according to W. R. Irwin, who includes most traditional fairy tales in this category [105].

ANTINOMIES. See BINARY OPPOSITION.

ANTI-QUEST. Narrative in which one or more major conventions of the Quest* motif is reversed. According to Christine Brooke-Rose, *The Odyssey* is an anti-quest in that it concerns adventures of a homeward, rather than an outward, journey, and *The Lord of the Rings* is an anti-quest since it involves disposing of a treasure rather than gaining one [38].

ANTI-SCIENCE FICTION. Damon Knight's description of novels (specifically *The Power* by Frank Robinson and *The Shrinking Man* by Richard Matheson, both published in 1956) characterized by "a turning away, not merely from the standard props of science fiction (which are retained as vestiges) but from the habits of thought and belief which underlie science itself." Such works may appeal to popular fears and concerns about science, but lack the rigor of thought that some regard as characteristic of true science fiction [110]. Others have suggested the term Sci-Fi* for such works, which are more often associated with film and television than with modern science fiction literature. More recently, "anti-science fiction" has been used by Robert Scholes and Eric Rabkin to describe a group of works in which some of the conventions of science fiction are used to present arguments in opposition to Scientism,* notably the space novels of C. S. Lewis [174]. See also ANTISCIENTISM.

ANTISCIENTISM. Used loosely by a number of writers on science fiction to refer to everything from the attitudes toward science revealed in grade B science fiction films to the general carelessness about scientific matters in an author such as Ray Bradbury to the specific attacks upon scientific ideology in works such as C. S. Lewis' *That Hideous Strength* (1946). The latter usage is probably the most precise, since it refers to a work specifically set in opposition to a brand of Scientism* (in Lewis' case, that represented by the work of J. B. S. Haldane [121]). An author such as Bradbury may be said to be "anti-science" when he expresses, as he does in several early stories, a skepticism or disapproval of the general pattern of scientific thought or the behavior of scientists, but "antiscientism" more properly implies an opposition to a specific ideology of science.

ANTI-UTOPIA. A satirical or ironic treatment of utopian themes, sometimes contrasted with dystopia (Gr., "the bad place"), which is taken to mean narratives of undesirable societies that are not specifically satirical of assumptions in utopian fiction. While anti-utopian narratives may occasionally be joined with conventions of fantasy (as in George Orwell's *Animal Farm*, 1945), such narratives are more often regarded as belonging to the traditions of utopian literature. John Huntington has argued for a clear distinction between dystopia and anti-utopia; while utopian/dystopian works are built around good or bad principles and provide the bases for coherently imagined societies that the author wants to promote or warn against, anti-utopia, in Huntington's terms, refers to "a type of skeptical imagining that is opposed to the consistencies of utopia-dystopia," or that questions the very assumptions concerning human behavior that utopias and dystopias promote [104].

APOCALYPTIC LITERATURE. Traditionally, religious or millenial literature dealing with the end of the world and the establishment of a new order. (The Greek *apokalupsis* means literally an "unveiling," especially of future events or of invisible realms.) "Apocalypse" has gained currency as a critical term through the work of George Snell, D. H. Lawrence, R. W. B. Lewis, Ihab Hassan, M. H. Abrams, Northrop Frye, Frank Kermode, and—especially in relation to fantastic literature—David Ketterer. While some of these critics, such as Hassan, have identified apocalyptic literature with a kind of existential confrontation with meaninglessness, others, such as Frye, have emphasized the visionary aspect of the term; Frye's definition of apocalypse, for example, is "the imaginative conception of the whole of nature as the content of an infinite and eternal living body, which if not human, is closer to being human than to being inanimate" [92]. Ketterer argues that apocalyptic literature deals with "the creation of other worlds which exist, on the literal level, in a credible relationship . . . with the 'real' world, thereby causing a metaphorical destruction of that 'real' world in the reader's head" [108]. Fantasy is thus distinguished from apocalyptic literature in that it lacks such a "credible relationship," while mimetic literature attempts to represent the "real" world itself. Earlier critics, such as Gerald Heard, had similarly identified science fiction as "the apocalyptic literature of our particular and culminating epoch of crisis" [35], but in popular parlance the term has most often been used to describe fiction in which an actual apocalypse is portrayed, such as nuclear war. See also POST-HOLOCAUST.

APPLIED FANTASY. Fantasies in which motives such as political satire or social consciousness raising play a significant part; specifically used by Robert Crossley to refer to utopian romances that "apply" fantastic devices toward social or philosophical ends [171].

ARCANOLOGY. The study of mysterious or initiatory bodies of knowledge, commonly a feature of fantasy or supernatural narratives. Examples might include the use of Rosicrucian ideas in Edward Bulwer-Lytton's *A Strange Story* (1861) or the Celtic "weirdin" in Charles de Lint's *Moonheart* (1984). See also OCCULT FICTION.

ARCHETYPE. C. G. Jung's notion of prototypical images providing evidence of a collective unconscious ("Archetypes of the Collective Unconscious," 1934). Jung's concept, modified by later writers, has provided an intellectual framework for discussing many of the common images and themes in fantasy narratives (for example, the wise woman, the heroic quest) and has arguably influenced a number of modern fantasy authors.

ARTIFICTION. Term coined by Brian W. Aldiss (in ''Three Revolutionary Enigmas,'' 1980) apparently as a portmanteau of ''artifice'' and ''fiction'' and referring to highly structured and self-conscious works of fiction [96]. See also FABULATION.

AUGMENTED WORLD. See ADDITIVE WORLD.

AUTOPLASTIC. See ALLOPLASTIC.

B

BEAST-FABLE. A Fable* characterized by animals who talk and behave as humans. Although excluded from the genre of fairy tales by Tolkien and others, the beast-fable has provided the basis not only of major children's fantasies such as Kenneth Grahame's *The Wind in the Willows* (1908) but in recent years of adult fantasies such as Richard Adams' *Watership Down* (1972). See also ANIMAL FANTASY.

BEM. A fan term meaning "bug-eyed monster" and used to signal a particularly sensational variety of (usually) Pulp* science fiction. Unlike most fan terminology, the term has achieved fairly wide usage in critical and historical literature about science fiction as well, and is sometimes used as a signal word to represent conventions of early pulp science fiction.

BESTSELLER. Often used disparagingly by genre writers, and often to refer to "mainstream" books which achieve a measure of success perceived inaccessible to Ghetto* authors. In fact, bestseller lists, which first became popular in the 1920s following their introduction by *The Bookman* in 1895, have always been skewed against popular genres, and "bestseller" has come to mean merely a book appearing on one of these lists. But such lists long ignored genre and paperback fiction and for years were weighted heavily in favor of urban areas and the Northeast in particular. In more recent years, such lists have employed more sophisticated polling techniques (the *New York Times Book Review*, for example, claims to sample not only 2,000 bookstores but a statistically weighted sample of over 40,000 retail outlets of various kinds), but questions remain as to the accuracy of reporting and the biases inherent in the sample. The science fiction community was not long in picking up the implications of this bias and now compiles its own bestseller lists based on reports from mass market and specialty bookstores, the latter of which are frequently ignored in more general compilations. (See, for example, the lists published monthly in the science fiction newsmagazine *Locus*.) While occasional science fiction or fantasy works by well-known authors such as Arthur C. Clarke or Stephen King regularly appear on national bestseller lists, the genre lists are as a rule more dependable in identifying trends and popular new authors. As a critical term, "bestseller" retains some of its disparaging overtones both within and without the genre, usually referring to the perceived tendency of such works to reinforce middle-class values, clarify or exploit ideas already in general circulation, and provide accessible patterns of emotion and character.

BINARY OPPOSITION. A common technique used in Structuralist* criticism and scholarship, popularized in language study by A. J. Greimas, in anthropology by Claude Levi-Strauss, and in literary criticism by Roland Barthes. Binary oppositions or antinomies are key structural units that define the semantic space within which a given myth or tale operates and around which other elements may be organized. Both Mark Rose and Gary K. Wolfe have identified such oppositions which they believe are central to science fiction; in Rose, it is the human/nonhuman opposition [160], while in Wolfe it is the opposition of known and unknown [208]. Narratives built around such oppositions often seek to resolve or make acceptable to the reader the opposition, which is itself usually regarded as irreducible.

BLUE BOOKS. Popular novels, similar to Penny Dreadfuls,* which gained popularity in early nineteenth-century England by reprinting abridgements of Gothic* novels or cheap imitations; thus, early precursors of the Pulp* magazines.

BLURB. Promotional copy written on the dust covers of hardbound books and on the front and back covers and front page of paperbacks. Although blurbs are most often written by promotional staff or freelance public relations writers, they often include quotations from reviews or specially solicited praise from fellow authors—to the extent that some well-known authors have gained reputations for excessive generosity in lending their names to the efforts of lesser known authors. Given the overall importance of marketing and packaging to the audience's perceptions of popular literature, blurbs can also be revealing clues to the changing attitudes toward genres such as science fiction or fantasy. One of the earliest science fiction anthologies, for example (Donald A. Wollheim's *The Pocket Book of Science Fiction*, 1943), featured a blurb that characterized the contents as belonging to "that realm of superscience where non-scientists try to anticipate science." Wollheim's later anthology *The Portable Novels of Science* (1945) avoided the term "science fiction" on the jacket cover by calling the contents "novels of scientific speculation," while an early Judith Merril anthology disguised the science fiction contents as "a different kind of mystery thrill" and a popular anthology by Orson Welles used the term "interplanetary stories." Similarly, a 1944 fantasy anthology from Penguin disguised its contents as humor ("yarns based on DELIGHTFUL PHANTASY") despite the inclusion of such relatively grim tales as Jack London's "The Scarlet Plague." By the early 1950s, however, the paperback market for science fiction at least (fantasy would emerge later) became sufficiently strong that such evasive blurb copy was replaced by enthusiastic and frequent use of the term "science fiction" (except in the case of novels, such as Philip Wylie's *Tomorrow!*, 1954, directed at a wider market) and this quickly led to complete lines of science fiction titles from Doubleday, Ballantine, and other publishers. (It is interesting to note, however, that after the success of Ray Bradbury's *The Martian Chronicles*, 1950, which was labeled "Doubleday Science Fiction," his second book for Doubleday, *The Illustrated Man*, 1951, was not identified as science fiction anywhere on the jacket.) As the market for science fiction grew and diversified, blurbs came more to reflect what was known of reader interest and consequently somewhat less hysterical. A common technique (still in use, although perhaps more in fantasy) was to compare the work with an acknowledged classic or a recent bestseller; reprints often became instant classics themselves. Although most serious readers claim not to be strongly influenced by blurbs, there is much to suggest that, along with cover design, they are crucial in capturing the casual reader and thus in influencing sales figures, which in turn of course influence patterns of manuscript development and acquisition.

BOUND MOTIF. See MOTIF.

"BUSINESS." A term used by some writers and editors, including Lin Carter, to describe certain pyrotechnic effects or "gimmicks" (the casting of a spell, the sudden transformation of a landscape, etc.) which are thought to give fantasy much of its appeal to readers [47].

C

CACOTOPIA. See KAKOTOPIA.

CAMPBELL ERA. The period in the history of science fiction characterized by the dominant influence of John W. Campbell, Jr. Campbell edited *Astounding Science Fiction* from September 1937 until his death in 1971, and the period of his influence is widely called the "Campbell era," just as fiction in the style of this period is often even today called "Campbellian." Such fiction is generally characterized by realistic depiction of carefully worked out science fictional ideas, often with as much attention paid to the details of the imaginary society as to the specific scientific concept being addressed, and necessary exposition worked into the fabric of the narrative. As a historical term, however, "Campbell era" is a bit slippery; Isaac Asimov used it to refer only to the period 1938–1945 (see also Adventure Dominant*) [14], while later writers would extend it to 1949 or 1950 (when the appearance of *Galaxy* and *The Magazine of Fantasy and Science Fiction* began to challenge the dominance of *Astounding*). Still other writers, referring particularly to the history of *Astounding*, have used the term to encompass the entire period of Campbell's editorship.

CAUTIONARY TALE. A story intended more as a warning than as an extrapolation or as pure satire, usually focusing on present social, political, or economic trends that the author feels to be dangerous in some way. The most familiar example is probably George Orwell's *1984* (1949), which also illustrates the importance of the difference between cautionary tales and Predictions.* Orwell was disturbed in the months after the novel appeared at the extent to which reviewers and readers seemed to overlook the rhetorical strategy of the cautionary tale and instead read the novel as a straightforward attempt at Anticipation.*

CHRISTIAN FANTASY. "Works of High Fantasy* whose contents reflect Christian beliefs and attitudes," according to Kenneth J. Zahorski and Robert H. Boyer [33].

CHRONOTOPE. The connection between temporal and spatial relationships within the plot structure of a work of narrative art. The word was borrowed from Mikhail Bakhtin by Darko Suvin as a means of characterizing the Novum* which he argues is a defining factor in the ideational structure of science fiction [187].

CINEFANTASTIC. Film or television science fiction and fantasy; the term has been used occasionally by critics like Rosemary Jackson [106] and, as *Cinefantastique*, as the title of a journal on this topic.

CLASSICAL FANTASY. Often used to refer to fantasy narratives based on classical sources (such as novels by Thomas Burnett Swann). However, Algis Budrys used this term to draw a distinction between earlier literary traditions and popular genre fantasy, or Newsstand Fantasy* [41].

CLASS OF 1951. A group of young writers of varying backgrounds, most with some university education, who began publishing science fiction around 1951, mostly in *Galaxy*. The term is suggested by Algis Budrys, who was a member of this group along with Michael Shaara, Robert Sheckley, Philip K. Dick, and others [43].

CLOSED SYSTEM. See SYSTEMS MODEL.

COGNITION. See COGNITIVE ESTRANGEMENT.

COGNITIVE ESTRANGEMENT. Widely quoted term from Darko Suvin describing the defining characteristic of science fiction, which Suvin sees as estranged from the naturalistic world but cognitively connected to it. "Noncognitive estrangement," according to this scheme, would include myths, folktales, and fantasies which are neither naturalistic nor cognitively linked to the natural world. Suvin argues that the defining characteristics of science fiction are Estrangement* and "cognition," the latter referring to those elements of variability and detail drawn from the empirical environment that establish a link between the experienced world of the reader and the world of the work of fiction; a flying carpet, therefore, would violate this principle of cognition [187].

COINCIDENCE OF OPPOSITIES. Jungian term referring to the dissolution of the defining barriers between antitheses, as portrayed in myth. For example, myths and folktales may blur the boundaries between animate and inanimate, living and dead, etc. Casey Fredericks has used the term in discussing the relationship of myth to science fiction and fantasy narratives [89].

COLLECTIVE UNCONSCIOUS. C. G. Jung's notion of a part of the unconscious which is not personally acquired, but rather is inherited through ancient memories or Archetypes* ("Archetypes of the Collective Unconscious," 1934). The idea is related to the Freudian concept of "racial memory" (*Moses and Monotheism*, 1939) and has often been cited in psychological discussions both of the appeal of fantastic literature and of the origins and meanings of its characteristic conventions and images.

COMIC FANTASY. In the broadest sense, any fantasy with humorous intent; more specifically, one of two broad classes of fantasy described by C. N. Manlove in his 1975 study *Modern Fantasy*. "Comic" or Escapist* fantasy, according to Manlove, is that which lacks the deeper meaning or serious purpose of Imaginative Fantasy* [132].

COMIC INFERNO. Oft-quoted phrase coined by Kingsley Amis to describe humorous satirical dystopias or Anti-Utopias* characterized by a "jesting tone" and "consistent and concrete elaboration." Examples would be the satirical novels of Frederik Pohl and C. M. Kornbluth, such as *The Space Merchants* (1953) [8].

COMIC SCIENCE FICTION. Humor has been a consistent substrain of science fiction, which provides ample opportunities for the kind of unexpected juxtapositions that often give rise to it. As a critical term, however, "comic" has been used in a somewhat more specialized sense by Donald M. Hassler, who sees it as a dislocation characteristic of science fiction, but related to earlier modes of irony and narrative indeterminacy; his science fiction examples include Ursula Le Guin, Theodore Sturgeon, and Hal Clement [100].

CONCEALED ENVIRONMENT. Term attributed to Christopher Priest which describes a science fiction narrative in which the true nature of the setting is initially unknown to the characters and often to the reader; the device is particularly common in "generation starship" tales such as Robert A. Heinlein's "Universe" (1941) [96].

CONCEPTUAL BREAKTHROUGH. Peter Nicholls has identified this as one of the central themes of science fiction, and the most characteristic manner in which science fiction deals with the quest for knowledge which is the genre's "central vision." Essentially, he describes the theme in terms of the "paradigms" of scientific thought as outlined by Thomas Kuhn in his study *The Structure of Scientific Revolutions* (1962): A particular world view or framework for scientific thought is accepted until anomalies generate crises that can only be resolved through acceptance of a new framework or paradigm. Stories in which the inhabitants of a world act on false or incomplete information about that world (such as Heinlein's "Universe") or in which some inexplicable form of transcendental knowledge is gained (such as Stanley Kubrick and Arthur C. Clarke's *2001*) are among the kinds of works Nicholls identifies as employing this theme [144]. See also PARADIGM.

CONCRETE MYTH. Mythic narrative generated from an abstract social or scientific idea, according to Robert M. Philmus, who argues that science fiction "generates its mythic fantasies by taking literally, and dramatizing, the metaphors expressive of those ideas that define, at least in part, the beliefs and nature of the social order" [150]. See also DISPLACEMENT; MYTH.

CONDENSED NOVEL. J. G. Ballard's term for a series of short works of fiction (collected in *The Atrocity Exhibition*, 1970) which explore in elliptical and fragmented form various aspects of contemporary popular culture and history. In more general usage, seldom relevant to fantastic literature, the term refers to severely edited novels, such as those published over a period of years by *Reader's Digest* Magazine. While such condensed or shortened novels have not been uncommon in the history of science fiction (nearly all the "Galaxy Novels" published in the early 1950s, as well as many paperbacks, were edited to a specific length), the term itself has seldom been used to describe them. Finally, the term was used by Bret Harte for an 1867 collection of short parodies of popular novelists of the day.

CONDITIONAL JOY. A term coined for "the pleasure of pedantry" by G. K. Chesterton in his 1908 study *Orthodoxy*, "The Doctrine of Conditional Joy" refers to the common motif in fairy tales of offering a great boon to the protagonist on the condition of not violating a seemingly arbitrary taboo. Chesterton argues that this reveals how the natural laws of Faerie* are determined by human action rather than by "scientific fatalism" [50].

CONSENSUS FUTURE HISTORY. See COSMOGONY.

CONSENSUS REALITY. The "real world," or Zero World,* whose norms provide the frame of reference for fantastic or impossible events in a narrative [102].

CONSOLATION. J. R. R. Tolkien's term, in "On Fairy Stories" (1947), for the effect of the "happy ending" or Eucatastrophe,* and one of the four principal functions of fairy stories, along with Fantasy,* Recovery,* and Escape* [194]. Psychoanalysts such as Bruno Bettelheim have argued that this may be among the most significant functions of fairy tales, in that it directly addresses the fear of abandonment, or "separation anxiety," experienced by young children [26].

CONTE PHILOSOPHIQUE. Genre developed in eighteenth-century France as a means of popularizing philosophical notions through action and style, with character and complex plot development subservient. Frequently such tales made use of fantastic events or situations, and while the genre's most famous practitioner is undoubtedly Voltaire (*Zadig*, 1747; *Micromégas*, 1750; *Candide*, 1758), it also contributed to the development of such science fiction themes as the futuristic romance (Louis Sébastien Mercier's *L'An deus mille quatre cent quarante*, 1771, translated as *Memoirs of the Year Two Thousand Five Hundred*) or the Lost race* (Restif de la Bretonne's *La Découverte australe*, 1781).

CONTINUUM OF THE FANTASTIC. A means proposed by Eric S. Rabkin to differentiate among subgenres of the fantastic by arranging works according to the degree of their fantastic content. On the broadest scale, Rabkin suggests a series of works with Henry James' *The Ambassadors* (1903) at one end and Lewis Carroll's *Alice in Wonderland* (1865) at the other; within fantastic genres, a series with Isaac Asimov's *I, Robot* (1950) at one end and David Lindsay's *A Voyage to Arcturus* (1920) at the other might help to clarify the point at which science fiction shades into fantasy [156].

CONTRANATURAL FICTION. Fiction presenting "a world view that is in direct opposition to that of materialism," according to Everett F. Bleiler [27].

CONTRASTIVE WORLD. A fictional world that comments on reality by presenting two more limited realities in contrast to one another. Kathryn Hume uses this term, along with Additive World* and Subtractive World,* to describe the means by which narratives may comment on reality [102].

COSMIC DISASTER STORY. Kingsley Amis' phrase for a long-popular tradition of science fiction and fantasy stories that deal with world- or even universe-threatening disasters brought on by natural forces (as in John Christopher's *No Blade of Grass*, 1956, which Amis discusses) or by human folly (as in numerous nuclear war tales; see Post-Holocaust*). Amis argues that such tales differ from other science fiction in that they bear no real extrapolative or analogical relationship with our own society, but instead may be used to explore propositions about the nature of society and human interaction. (Amis does not mention the nature of reality, which came increasingly to be of central concern in J. G. Ballard's series of disaster novels such as *The Crystal World*, 1966.) Such works are perhaps more commonly referred to simply as "disaster stories" or "disaster novels" [8]. See also APOCALYPTIC LITERATURE; ESCHATOLOGICAL ROMANCE.

COSMIC VOYAGE. Those works of the Imaginary Voyage* genre which concern voyages to other worlds and which characteristically focus as much on the voyage itself as on the nature of the other world, according to Marjorie Hope Nicolson [145]. Mark Hillegas later distinguished this from Space Fiction,* which is set on other worlds but with little or no concern for how characters got there [54].

COSMOGONY. An account or theory of the origin of the universe. While cosmogony has played a significant enough thematic role in many works of science fiction and fantasy (with a few novels, such as C. S. Lewis' *The Magician's Nephew*, 1955, openly cosmogonic in nature), the word has come to have a rather odd meaning in discussions of science fiction through its idiosyncratic use by Donald A. Wollheim to describe a "consensus" Future History* as revealed in science fiction of the 1940s and 1950s. Wollheim's eight-stage "cosmogony" includes the exploration of the moon and planets, travel to the stars, three stages of a galactic empire, an interregnum following the fall of the empire, a permanent galactic civilization, and finally a "Challenge to God." While interesting as a means of revealing the assumptions and expectations of writers and readers during an important period in the history of science fiction, this "consensus" depends heavily upon writers who published in *Astounding Science Fiction*, especially Isaac Asimov, and is of course not a "cosmogony" at all in the usual sense of the term [212].

COSMOLOGY. The structure and meaning of the physical universe as revealed through a given system of thought. The narrative action of most fantasy narratives implies such a cosmology, and a number of authors (such as J. R. R. Tolkien) have carefully constructed such cosmological systems as underpinning for the narratives themselves. In a few cases, such as Tolkien's *Silmarillion* (1977), the cosmology virtually becomes the narrative. In science fiction study, the term usually refers to the science of cosmology, which studies the structure and physical nature of the universe. This science, always highly speculative and theoretical, has been a natural breeding ground for a variety of popular science fiction themes, including parallel worlds, worlds within worlds, time travel, relativity effects, and Conceptual Breakthroughs,* such as narratives of Concealed Environments* which describe societies with incomplete or erroneous cosmological theories who eventually discover the true nature of the universe (for example, Robert A. Heinlein's "Universe," 1941).

COSMOTROPISM. Another odd term from Donald A. Wollheim (see Cosmogony*), this time to describe the "outward urge" toward space exploration, which Wollheim sees as a principle of human nature that is addressed only by science fiction [212].

COSY CATASTROPHE. Coined by Brian W. Aldiss to describe a group of primarily British cosmic disaster stories characterized by their preoccupation with middle-class environments and characters [1].

CRITIC, CRITICISM. As with many popular genres that evolved without much serious critical attention outside the letter and review columns of magazines or the commentary of the fan press, science fiction has experienced some confusion over the meaning of the term "critic." Many authors and fans still use the terms "critic" and "criticism" interchangeably with "reviewer" and "review," and indeed much of the most valuable criticism of the genre has come from reviewers such as Damon Knight or Algis Budrys. "Critic" in the more literary sense of a commentator upon a text or group of texts is thus of comparatively recent vintage. Sometimes the phrase is qualified as "academic critic," to distinguish professional scholars from fan or writer critics. Perhaps because of the relative lack of a scholarly humanistic tradition in the field, some naive assumptions remain; for example, that a critic is one who finds fault, that the role of a "critic" is to recommend books for purchase, that criticism is inevitably evaluative, etc. Partly for this reason, there persists a noticeable gap between the assumptions of those who approach the genre from the traditions of humanistic scholarship and those who approach it from the perspectives of fans or professional authors.

CYBERPUNK. Used to describe a group of young science fiction writers who emerged in the mid–1980s with narratives characterized by a combination of advanced scientific concepts (especially relating to cybernetics), New Wave* narrative techniques, and the fast-paced plotting

characteristic of more traditional science fiction. The term may have
been coined by Gardner Dozois, and alternative terms which have been
suggested include "neuromantic" and "mirrorshade school." The most
often cited examples include William Gibson's novel *Neuromancer* (1984)
and Bruce Sterling's *Schismatrix* (1985).

D

DARK FANTASY. Term sometimes used interchangeably with Gothic*
fantasy.

DAYDREAM. See REVERIE.

DECENTRATION. See ESTRANGEMENT.

DEFAMILIARIZATION. See ESTRANGEMENT.

DEMONIC. Originally used to refer to a supernatural or diabolical force,
"demonic" has gradually come to refer to the darker aspects of character
or nature in fantastic literature. Rosemary Jackson traces this change
in meaning of the term, associating it with the concept of the Other*
as a "manifestation of unconscious desire" and citing Mary Shelley's
Frankenstein as among the earliest works giving evidence of the
internalization of the demonic [106].

DEMONIC AGENT. According to Thomas H. Keeling, a figure
characteristic of Gothic* narratives "whose obsession (or 'possession')
radically restricts [his] vision and behavior." Such figures may in fact
be possessed by outside forces, which in turn may be supernatural (as
in the case of the early Gothic) or merely alien (as in the case of demonic
agents in later science fiction narratives; Keeling cites works by Philip
K. Dick as examples, although the theme of "possession" by an alien
intelligence is one of the most persistent traditions of popular science
fiction). The demonic agent, however, is according to Keeling a defining
factor only in the gothic [181].

DEMONSTRATION POLEMIC. Used by Joe De Bolt and John R. Pfeiffer as a general term to describe that large subgenre of fantastic literature, including Utopias* and dystopias, which seek to dramatize a particular "polemical" point of view through dramatic "demonstration" [22]. See also APPLIED FANTASY.

DESIRE. A term sometimes used to describe the wish-fulfillment aspect of the appeal of fantasy, and sometimes used (as by Rosemary Jackson [106]) to characterize the nature of language in fantasy narratives, as opposed to the more representational language of conventional narratives. Leo Bersani's use of this term (in *A Future for Astyanix: Character and Desire in Literature*, 1976), suggests that it refers to a generalized yearning for something beyond the real, and thus might in part account for the disintegration of realistic structures of character and narrative that is often found in fantasy. The term has been used of science fiction as well, notably in Boris Eizykman's *Science Fiction et capitalisme* (1974), again with the implication of subverting dominant social structures through idealization of the possible. Much contemporary use of the term derives from the work of French psychoanalyst Jacques Lacan, and in particular his discussions of desire in its relationships to fantasy and to the "Other."*

DIGEST. Since 1922 and the founding of *Reader's Digest, digest* has generally referred to magazines that present abridged or summarized reprint articles on various topics; in science fiction and fantasy, however, the term has come to refer exclusively to the trim size of the magazines that became dominant in the 1950s, usually 5 1/4″ × 7 1/2″ or 5 1/2″ × 7 1/2″. *Astounding Science Fiction* was the first major science fiction magazine to shift to digest size, in 1943, and often the term is used in contrast with Pulp* magazines, which usually measured 7″ × 10″. In fact, however, some digest size magazines (such as *Other Worlds*) were printed on pulp paper stock in the later 1940s and early 1950s.

DIME NOVEL. Paperback booklets which reached their height of popularity in the United States in the 1880s and 1890s. Although often selling for less than a dime and almost never long enough to be considered true novels, these popular series of adventure stories are important to the history of science fiction not only as precursors of the Pulps,* but because of the science fiction that sometimes appeared in them, probably most notably in the "Frank Reade, Jr." stories of Luis Senarens.

DISASTER NOVEL. See COSMIC DISASTER STORY.

DISCONTINUITY. Sometimes used in describing a "break" between an imagined science fiction world and our own, which renders the imagined world "discontinuous" from an Extrapolated* present; for example, the sudden and unlikely growth in human intelligence in Poul Anderson's *Brain Wave* (1954) renders his imagined world discontinuous from our own. The term has also been invoked in science fiction study in the sense proposed by Morse Peckham in *Man's Rage for Chaos: Biology, Behavior, and the Arts* (1962), where he wrote of "perceptual discontinuities" in the visual arts which force the viewer to rethink the possibilities of art in order to respond to a radically new aesthetic work [89].

DISENCHANTMENT. According to Theodore Ziolkowski, certain fantastic images or icons such as magic mirrors or haunted portraits, have undergone a process of "disenchantment" during the last two centuries of literary history, becoming transformed from what Todorov [193] might call the Marvelous* to rationalized or psychological images and finally to parody and satire [216].

DIS-EXPECTED. Elements in a narrative "which the text had diverted one from thinking about but which, it later turns out, are in perfect keeping with the ground rules of the narrative," according to Eric S. Rabkin, who views such elements (characteristic of jokes) as more closely allied to the fantastic than merely unexpected events, but not so characteristic as the Anti-Expected* [156].

DISPLACEMENT. Technique by which science fiction achieves a fantastic "state of affairs" by "a deflection of reality into myth, and especially myth derived by dramatizing the metaphoric substance of various models of reality," according to Robert M. Philmus [150].

DISTANCE MARKER. A "textual element that allows us to measure the distance between the unfamiliar and the familiar worlds" in a work of fantastic fiction, according to Mark Rose. When H. G. Wells' time traveler finds artifacts of his own age in *The Time Machine* (1895), the discovery serves as a "distance marker" between that future world and the world of Wells' readers [160].

DOMESTICATION. Term used by H. G. Wells to describe the technique whereby the primary "magic trick" of a fantastic narrative is made believable and acceptable to the reader. Casey Fredericks has similarly suggested that a function of science fiction is that of "domesticating the unknown," that is, providing a rationale for a non-naturalistic environment or set of norms by showing how such elements can be accounted for by rational means [89, 203].

DOPPELGÄNGER. The theme of the double or alter ego. A staple of fantasy since the early nineteenth century, the *doppelgänger* was popularized initially in Germany by such authors as Jean Paul Richter and E. T. A. Hoffmann and later in the United States and England by Edgar Allan Poe and Robert Louis Stevenson. A number of science fiction themes have also made use of this convention, including the time-travel story, robot tales, and stories, such as those of Philip K. Dick, that question the nature of reality itself.

DOUBLE. See DOPPELGÄNGER.

DREAM LITERATURE. Joanna Russ' term for literature that appears to be the expression of daydreaming in its fondness for the "ineffable and inexpressible"; citing David Lindsay's *A Voyage to Arcturus* (1920) as an example, she condemns such literature as "thin and schematic" [164].

DREAM STORY. Waggoner's term for a story that reproduces a dream experience, such as *Alice in Wonderland* [199]. J. R. R. Tolkien excludes such works from consideration as fairy stories since they cheat the realization of "imagined wonder" [194].

DREAM-WORLD STORY. A fantasy set entirely in a Secondary World.* Damon Knight, writing in 1953 about Fletcher Pratt's "The Blue Star" (1952), used this term and defined it as a story in which "the dream-world must be completely insular, self-contained, having no point of contact with the mundane universe either in space or in time"—in other words, something quite similar to what is today more often called High Fantasy.* Ironically, writing only a year before J. R. R. Tolkien's famous trilogy began to appear, Knight complained that this genre had become "so rare nowadays I was beginning to think it was extinct" [110].

DYSCATASTROPHE. See EUCATASTROPHE.

DYSTOPIA. See ANTI-UTOPIA.

E

EASTERN TALE. See ORIENTAL TALE.

ECOLOGY. The study of the relationships between organisms or societies and their natural environments. "Literary ecology" was a term proposed by Joseph Meeker (*The Comedy of Survival: Studies in Literary Ecology*, 1974) to suggest that literature both reflects and forms our attitudes about nature, even in such broad outlines as tragedy and comedy. Don D. Elgin has applied this approach to fantasy narratives, which he sees as partaking of a healthier comic perspective [80].

ECSTASY. Poetic transport or visionary fancy, in its most common usage. The term is of particular interest in the study of fantasy and supernatural fiction, however, because of Arthur Machen's conception of "fine literature" as a means of communicating or leading the reader toward ecstasy (*Hieroglyphics*, 1902), by which Machen seems to have meant a whole complex of emotions—"wonder, awe, mystery, sense of the unknown, desire for the unknown"—which are associated with inner or deeper realities and which later writers and critics have often identified as some of the key effects of fantastic literature [127]. See also DESIRE; SUBLIME; WONDER.

EDENISM. A persistent romantic strain in Eschatological* or Cosmic Disaster* fiction, as described by W. Warren Wagar. Specifically, Wagar refers to the tendency to portray apocalypse as a means of returning to a more desirable, simpler, Edenic style of life. His examples include William Morris' *News from Nowhere* (1890), Ray Bradbury's *The Martian Chronicles* (1950), and Russell Hoban's *Riddley Walker* (1980) [198]. See also PRIMITIVISM.

EMPATHY. From the German critic Hermann Lotze's *Einfühlung* (literally, "feeling into") and used to refer to the reader's identification with an object, animal, or person. While much recent scholarship focuses on the interpersonal aspect of empathy, fantasy may achieve this end through literal transformations of its protagonists; hence, according to Ann Swinfen, empathy is the "dominant mode" by which fantasy enhances the "primary sense perceptions" [189].

ENCHANTMENT. "The elvish craft" to which fantasy aspires, according to J. R. R. Tolkien, who argues that this is the emotional function of Sub-Creation* [194].

ENTROPIC ROMANCE. Narratives set in the far future and concerning the gradual death of the planet, solar system, or universe through natural processes of entropy and the second law of thermodynamics. The term is used by W. Warren Wagar to describe such novels as William Hope Hodgson's *The Night Land* (1912) or Camille Flammarion's *The End of the World* (*La fin du monde*, 1880), and the tradition has persisted in genre science fiction with such tales as John W. Campbell, Jr.'s "Night" (1935) and Brian W. Aldiss' *Hothouse* (1962) [198].

ENVIRONMENTAL FICTION. Sometimes loosely used to refer to any fiction with an environmental theme (an extreme example might be Philip Wylie's 1972 *The End of the Dream*), but proposed by Brian W. Aldiss as a way of characterizing works that "deal with man in relation to his changing surroundings and abilities"—an arena in which "the greatest successes of science fiction" have taken place [1].

EPIC. A long narrative poem, usually dealing with the exploits of national heroes and often featuring fantastic events. In popular usage, however, the term has come to refer to almost any narrative on a grand scale, and Patrick Parrinder may be justified in his complaint that a "debased" use of the term is "one of the most regular features of the promotional material on SF put out by publishers and film companies" [149]. See also EPIC FABLES; EPIC FANTASY.

EPIC FABLES. Short works of science fiction in which "a single future crisis is portrayed with precision and economy," and that imply a future heroic age of epic proportions, according to Patrick Parrinder, who views such shorter works as generally more successful than longer attempts at epic narrative forms in science fiction, which he also refers to as "truncated epic" [181]. Parrinder's views reflect indirectly Edgar Allan Poe's earlier argument that poetry is essentially a discontinuous mode best suited for the achievement of particular effects, which led to a fragmentation of the epic form in poetry, with shorter poems implying a larger unwritten epic framework of which they are only a part. An example of such a technique in science fiction might be the work of Cordwainer Smith (Paul M. A. Linebarger), whose "Instrumentality of Mankind" stories imply a broader narrative that Linebarger never published.

EPIC FANTASY. Fantasy that shares characteristics common to the epic, such as elevated style, grandly heroic figures, vast settings, and supernatural intervention—all involved in a struggle in which some central cultural value or values are at stake. Publishers have come to use the term somewhat more loosely to describe almost any multivolume fantasy work.

ESCAPE. Popularly (and loosely) used to describe the appeal of much fantastic literature, and referring to the presumed function of such literature as a kind of psychological safety valve. Tolkien uses the term more specifically as one of the key functions of the fairy story, and argues that it is not so much an escape or flight from reality as a liberation *into* a wider reality: the "Escape of the Prisoner" as opposed to the "Flight of the Deserter" [194]. C. S. Lewis elaborates on this argument by emphasizing that "escape" is a criticism of the reader rather than the work, and that many readers might well "escape" into realistic fictions [120]. See also CONSOLATION; FANTASY; RECOVERY.

ESCHATOLOGICAL ROMANCE. A narrative concerned with last things—the end of a civilization, a species, the world, the entire universe. W. Warren Wagar includes in this subgenre a wide variety of Cosmic Disaster* stories as well as recent novels such as Doris Lessing's *The Memoirs of a Survivor* (1974) [198].

ESEMPLASTIC. Literally, Greek for "molding into unity." Samuel Taylor Coleridge (*Biographia Literaria*, 1817) described the Imagination's* ability to create unity from diversity as the "esemplastic power" [93].

ESTRANGED FICTION. Darko Suvin's term for works of fiction that, in opposition to "naturalistic fiction," pose radically different formal frameworks for the narrative, such as unverifiable characters, places, or events [187]. See also ESTRANGEMENT.

ESTRANGEMENT. Broadly, the gaining of new perspectives through devices of defamiliarization and distancing. First suggested as a critical term by the Russian Formalist Viktor Shklovsky in 1917 ("Isskusstvo kak priem," trans. 1965 as "Art and Technique"), "estrangement" came into common usage especially among Marxist critics following its usage by Bertolt Brecht during the 1930s. (Although the exact derivation of the term is complicated by the fact that Shklovsky's original *ostranenie* has been variantly translated as "defamiliarization" and Brecht's *Verfremdung* as "alienation," Darko Suvin combined these into the single "estrangement" in his study of science fiction.) Brecht argued that estrangement was a technique that allowed us to recognize a subject while at the same time making it seem unfamiliar ("Kleines Organon für das Theater," trans. 1964 as "A Brief Organon for the Theatre"), and Suvin argued that this is a defining technique of science fiction (see Cognitive Estrangement*) [187]. Casey Fredericks extended the term to include psychological adjustment to radically new systems of thinking, and compared it to the "decentration" of the psychology of Jean Piaget, the "perceptual discontinuity" of Morse Peckham's analysis of the visual arts, the "Paradigm* shift" of Thomas Kuhn's theory of the history of science, and the Recovery* aspect of J. R. R. Tolkien's discussion of fairy tales [89].

ETHICAL FANTASY. A fantasy, usually for children, characterized by didactic or values-oriented motives [136]. The term has also been used to describe fantasies that explore or develop ethical systems; Alexei and Cory Panshin, for example, characterized David Lindsay's *A Voyage to Arcturus* (1920) as an "ethical fantasy" [204].

EUCATASTROPHE. Tolkien's widely quoted term for the "happy ending" which he argues marks the true fairy tale and is associated with Joy*; as opposed to the "dyscatastrophe" of tragedy [194].

EUCHRONIAN. Literally, "happy time," and sometimes used in discussions of Utopian* or futuristic fiction to denote a period of (usually future) history characterized by prosperity, often resulting from technological advances. Although uncommon, the term does provide an alternative to the more ideologically loaded "utopia."

EVOLUTIONARY FANTASY. Term used by Brian Aldiss specifically to describe the work of Olaf Stapledon; by implication, it may also refer to any fantastic work whose time frame is sufficiently large to provide a dramatization of long-term evolutionary processes [1]. See also ENTROPIC ROMANCE.

EXCHANGE. A theory or social model which holds that exchanges of rewards, esteem, and so forth, are fundamental structuring forces in society. Exchange theory is associated in sociology with the work of George Homans and Peter Blau, and in anthropology with Marcel Mauss and Claude Levi-Strauss. The imaginary societies of science fiction and fantasy, then, must implicitly maintain some patterns of exchange to remain credible, and thus, some critics have argued (most notably Jeanne Murray Walker), exchange models constitute a valid approach to the analysis of such texts [200].

EXISTENTIAL FANTASY. In a general sense, any fantasy associated with the existential movement in philosophy and art, or the writers associated with that movement—Jean-Paul Sartre's *Les Jeux Sont Faits* (1947), for example. George E. Slusser, however, has suggested a broader meaning for the term, and uses it to identify a tendency in some modern fantasy toward opacity and nonreferentiality of images [182].

EXOLINGUISTICS. Coined presumably on the model of "exobiology" by Myra E. Barnes to describe the study of imaginary or extraterrestrial languages as concocted by writers of science fiction and fantasy [21]. See also Walter E. Meyers, *Aliens and Linguists* (1980) [133].

EXTRAORDINARY VOYAGE. See COSMIC VOYAGE; VOYAGES EXTRAORDINAIRES.

EXTRAPOLATION. Probably derived from "interpolation" and used by statisticians to refer to the process of predicting a value beyond a known series by detecting patterns within the series. Extended into the social and natural sciences, "extrapolation" has become one of the most common characteristics cited in discussions and definitions of science fiction, and even provided the title for the field's first academic journal, founded in 1959. Generally, it is used to mean the technique of basing imaginary worlds or situations on existing ones through cognitive or rational means; a Satire,* therefore, may be based on extrapolation but need not be, since the relationship of the world of the satire to our own might be purely metaphorical. An example of an extrapolative science fiction satire is Frederik Pohl and C. M. Kornbluth's *The Space Merchants* (1952), in which a future society dominated by advertising agencies is clearly an outgrowth of trends visible in the early 1950s.

The term is closely allied with Speculative Fiction,* and one of its earliest important usages occurred in the Robert E. Heinlein essay in which he proposed the latter term: In the "speculative science fiction story," he wrote, "accepted science and established facts are extrapolated to produce a new situation, a new framework for human action" [84]. Perhaps in part because of its scholarly sound, the term quickly gained popularity, and by 1955 Basil Davenport could report that extrapolation was "a word that is almost as great a favorite in discussions of science fiction as 'space-warp' is in science fiction itself; it may be defined as 'plotting the curve' " [66]. While treating extrapolation as a defining characteristic of science fiction would seem to limit the genre to fiction of the future, critics have managed to adapt the word to include extrapolations about the past, about Alternate Worlds,* and about other favorite themes. Other critics, however, have argued for distinctions between "extrapolative" and "nonextrapolative" kinds of science fiction narratives, while still others have expressed hope that the term might be banished altogether as restrictive and misleading.

F

FABLE. In its most general sense, any short, symbolic narrative pointing up a moral (a definition that would seem to include parables as well). Some folklorists argue that the fable is a variant of the etiological animal tale, that its purest form is the Beast-Fable,* and that the moral pointed up is always one of common sense. Science fiction has on occasion been touted as a means of presenting fables to less credulous modern audiences; as early as 1874 Robert Louis Stevenson argued that a "modern fable" would provide a "logical nexus between the moral expressed and the machinery employed to express it"—in other words, that modern readers seemed less willing to accept the pure fantastic as represented by earlier fables [150]. See also EPIC FABLE.

FABULATION. Robert Scholes' term for fiction that presents a world "radically discontinuous from," yet cognitively related to, our own. Popularized originally in Scholes' *The Fabulators* (1967), in which Scholes discussed such authors as Kurt Vonnegut, Jr., and John Barth, "fabulation" describes a kind of postrealistic work characterized by self-conscious attention to design, a sense of "art and joy," and didactic or satirical purpose [174, 175]. Scholes distinguishes two kinds of fabulation: "dogmatic," which operates out of a closed system and is roughly analogous to religious romances; and "speculative," which arises from humanistic tradition and incorporates the scientific romance [176].

FAERIE. "The realm or state in which fairies have their being," according to J. R. R. Tolkien, although he actually uses the term more broadly to describe the nature of the Secondary World* in general [194]. In general usage at least since Edmund Spenser's *The Faerie Queene* (1590) it refers to the realm of the fairies or the world of the supernatural; also spelled "faery."

FAERIE ROMANCE. A term used by George MacDonald as the subtitle of his 1858 fantasy *Phantastes*. The term was not widely adopted, and MacDonald subtitled his own later *Lilith* (1895) simply a "romance."

FAIRY TALE. In continuous use in English at least since 1750, but seldom used to refer exclusively to stories or legends dealing with fairies. Indeed, the most familiar tales, such as those collected by the Grimm brothers or Andrew Lang, feature few if any fairies. By the early nineteenth century, especially in Germany, the fairy tale or *Märchen** came to be valued as a dream-like story in which inexplicable supernatural occurrences and the frequent suspension of causality were taken as evidence of the "true vision" of the unconscious; this, together with the eventual liberation of the form from the Ghetto* of children's literature, has been cited by Manlove [132] and others as significant in the development of modern fantasy.

FANCY. In Samuel Taylor Coleridge's famous distinction between fancy and Imagination* (*Biographia Literaria*, 1817), the lesser "aggregative and associative" function to imagination's more fundamental "shaping and modifying" power. This dichotomy has survived in various forms in discussions of fantastic literature ever since. Leslie Stephen in 1879 described fancy as dealing with "superficial resemblances" while imagination deals with "the deeper truths that underlie them," and George MacDonald in 1893 argued that fancy represented "mere inventions" in the creation of secondary worlds while imagination represented "new embodiments of old truths." More recently, C. N. Manlove associates fancy with "comic" or "escapist" fantasy that carries no deeper meaning, as opposed to "imaginative" fantasy which seeks to invest the imagined world with a deeply felt sense of reality. He cites as examples of the former Milne, Morris, Dunsany, Eddison, and others; and of the latter Kingsley, MacDonald, Tolkien, Lewis, and Peake [132].

FANDOM. The organized readership of science fiction and, to a lesser extent, of other popular literatures. Sometimes carelessly used to refer to science fiction readership in general, fandom is more properly determined, as Algis Budrys points out, by participation in various "fannish" activities such as conventions and fanzines, and may or may not be related to the extent or nature of one's reading in the genre [43]. Although other popular genres such as the horror story or the detective novel have bodies of organized enthusiasts, "fandom" is usually confined to science fiction, and refers to a substantially smaller group than the readership at large of the genre. Often styled—or self-styled—a "subculture" because of its emphasis on jargon and ritualized behavior, fandom more closely approaches the definition of a folk culture, since by and large it does not constitute a complex of living conditions that set its members apart from the culture at large, but rather is a self-determined community whose members are deeply committed to it and whose "secrets" are passed along by oral tradition.

FANTASCIENCE. Cited by J. O. Bailey [19] as an early variant of "science fiction" (although the usage seems to be rare in English). In Italy, however, *Fantascienza* has been in common usage since 1952 to refer to science fiction, and provided the title of a study of the genre by Lino Aldani in 1962 (*La Fantascienza: Che Cos'e', Come e' Sorta, Dove Tende*).

FANTASIA. Generally, a work of art unrestricted by conventions of form or verisimilitude. The word has seldom been used in direct connection with fantastic literature, however, and Arnold Bennett even used it to refer to a series of light, satirical novels that were not in themselves fantasies. A more conventional usage is that of Brian Aldiss, who subtitled his 1970 novel *Barefoot in the Head* "A European Fantasia," presumably reflecting the variety of styles and forms used in that novel.

FANTASMATIC. The level of discourse associated with the fantastic, as opposed to the "noematic" discourse of more "realistic" writing. David Clayton describes the fantasmatic as "an investment of unconscious desire," but cautions that it is not the "unreal"—it exists only in relationship with the noematic, which "conceptually organizes the real"[57]. See also SUBJUNCTIVITY.

FANTASTIC. As a critical term, now frequently used in Tzvetan Todorov's sense of the uncertainty, when reading an apparently fantastic work, as to whether the impossible events are really occurring or whether they may be rationally explained. Once this uncertainty is resolved, the work belongs to the related genres of the Marvelous* (the supernatural accepted) or the Uncanny* (the supernatural explained) [193]. Many European scholars, however, have used the term in the sense first described by the French scholar Roger Caillois as a "break in reality," and thus almost diametrically opposed to the marvelous in that it is characterized by the intrusion of the supernatural or marvelous into an otherwise well-ordered world [162].

FANTASTIC OBJECTIVITY. The treatment of fantastic situations or events as objectively real, with no realistic "norms" presented from which the narrative may deviate in its introduction of the fantastic; T. E. Apter's example is the work of Franz Kafka [11].

FANTASTIC-PROPHETICAL AXIS. E. M. Forster's term for a broad range of fiction characterized by a "sense of mythology." His examples include Sterne and Melville as well as William Beckford and Walter de la Mare [87]. See also FANTASY; PROPHECY.

FANTASTIC ROMANCE. A "supergenre" defined by R. D. Mullen as "autonomous narratives depicting marvels as objectively real" and including the genres of science fiction, utopian fiction, and fantasy [141].

FANTASTIKA. Russian term for science fiction, shortened from *nauchnaia fantastika* and in use at least since 1925, when it was used as part of the subtitle of the magazine *World Pathfinder* [22].

FANTASY. A fictional narrative describing events that the reader believes to be Impossible.* This is the most commonly cited definition of literary fantasy, although it has been argued that such a definition places too great an emphasis on reader response and not enough on structural or thematic characteristics—not to mention its use of such an imprecise term as "impossible." A second problem with the term is the ongoing debate over whether it properly refers to a large narrative genre encompassing such subgenres as science fiction and horror, or whether these subgenres are in fact distinct. R. D. Mullen has attempted a compromise between these views by suggesting that fantasy is in fact a genre within the Supergenre* of Fantastic Romance* and is characterized by "autonomous narratives depicting supernatural, pseudonatural, and/ or sociocultural marvels as objectively real" [141]. Other definitions of fantasy:

E. M. Forster (1927): Fiction that "implies the supernatural, but need not express it" [87].

Herbert Read (1928): "The product of Fancy," in Coleridge's sense, and characterized by "objectivity and apparent arbitrariness" best exemplified by the fairy tale [159].

J. R. R. Tolkien (1947): "The most nearly pure form" of art, characterized by "arresting strangeness" and "freedom from the domination of observed 'fact' "; in other words, Sub-Creation* combined with "strangeness and wonder" [194].

Reginald Bretnor (1953): "Imaginative fiction in which no logical attempt is made, or needed, to justify the 'impossible' content of the story" [35].

Robert A. Heinlein (1957): A story that is "imaginary-and-not-possible" [67].

Rudolph B. Schmerl (1960): "The deliberate presentation of improbabilities through any one of four methods—the use of unverifiable time, place, characters, or devices—to a typical reader within a culture whose level of sophistication will enable that reader to recognize the improbabilities" [173].

Andrzej Zgorzelski (1967): "The breach of internal literary laws"; fantasy appears when "the internal laws of the fictional world are breached," as indicated by reactions of characters in the story [162].

Lloyd Alexander (1968): "Reality pretending to be a dream" [3].

Donald A. Wollheim (1971): "Pure fantasy is that branch of fantasy [in the whole of which Wollheim also includes science fiction and weird fiction] which, dealing with subjects recognizable as nonexistent and entirely imaginary, is rendered plausible by the reader's desire to accept it during the period of reading" [212].

Ursula K. Le Guin (1973): "An alternative technique for apprehending and coping with existence," characterized by a "pararational" "heightening of reality" and (in Freudian terms) primary process thinking [115].

Jane Mobley (1974): "A nonrational form . . . which arises from a world view essentially magical in its orientation. As a fiction, it requires the reader's entering an Other World and following a hero whose adventures take place in a reality far removed from the mundane reality of the reader's waking experience. This world is informed by Magic, and the reader must be willing to accept Magic as the central force without demanding or expecting mundane explanations" [134].

C. N. Manlove (1975): "A fiction evoking wonder and containing a substantial and irreducible element of supernatural or impossible worlds, beings or objects with which the mortal characters in the story or the readers become on at least partly familiar terms" [132].

W. R. Irwin (1976): "A story based on and controlled by an overt violation of what is generally accepted as possibility; it is the narrative result of transforming the condition contrary to fact into 'fact' itself" [105].

Eric S. Rabkin (1976): The "polar opposite" of reality; literature characterized by a "direct reversal of ground rules" from those of everyday existence" [156].

Marshall B. Tymn, Kenneth J. Zahorski, and Robert H. Boyer (1979): "Works in which nonrational phenomena play a significant part" (with "nonrational phenomena" further defined as those that "do not fall within human experience or accord with natural laws as we know them") [197].

Roger C. Schlobin (1979): "That corpus in which the impossible is primary in its quantity or centrality" [170].

Brian Attebery (1980): "Any narrative which includes as a significant part of its makeup some violation of what the author clearly believes to be natural law" [17].

Rosemary Jackson (1981): "A literature of desire, which seeks that which is experienced as absence or loss" [106].

Ann Swinfen (1984): "The essential ingredient of all fantasy is 'the marvellous', which will be regarded as anything outside the normal space-time continuum of the everyday world" [189].

Kathryn Hume (1984): "Any departure from consensus reality"; "the deliberate departure from the limits of what is usually accepted as real and normal" [102].

FANTASY ADAPTATION. See ADAPTATION.

FANTASY OF INNOCENCE. According to Irwin, a fantasy in which the innocence of children or childlike beings is informed or "organized" by principles such as energy or love [105].

FANTASY PASTORAL. See PASTORAL.

FANZINES. The periodical publications of Fandom,* which have ranged in size from postcards to magazines of professional quality. The term has sometimes been misused to include *any* periodical publications concerning science fiction or fantasy, including various scholarly journals.

FEMINIST SCIENCE FICTION. Variously applied to critical methodologies, to the ideological content of specific works, or to groups of works viewed in the context of a perceived commonality of outlook. Of these usages, the latter is the least precise, and has led to numerous attempts to trace a generic pattern from present feminist concerns back through the works of such authors as Leigh Brackett and Andre Norton. In the most extreme version of this usage, "feminist science fiction" might include practically any science fiction written by women, when viewed in terms of specific reading Protocols.* A considerably more narrow definition was offered by Barry Malzberg, who argued that "genuine" feminist science fiction would be that "in which women are perceived to react to events and internalize in a way which is neither a culturally received stereotype nor a merely male stereotype projected onto female characters" [129]. Such a definition, focusing almost exclusively on means of characterization, tends however to overlook the political concerns that have historically characterized feminist fiction. Although "feminism" is perhaps as hard to define as "science fiction" itself, there is nevertheless a long tradition of such self-consciously feminist fiction, and within this tradition there is a history of fantastic fiction, which includes such works as Charlotte Perkins Gilman's *Herland* (1915) and Joanna Russ' *The Female Man* (1975). The authors most commonly characterized as "feminist science fiction" authors—Russ, James Tiptree, Jr. (Alice Sheldon), Suzy McKee Charnas, Suzette Haden Elgin, and others—are often those who write in this intersection between feminist tradition and the science fiction genre.

FICTIONAL BIOGRAPHY. A work or series of works structured as an imaginary biography. A common tradition in both realistic and fantastic literature, the fictional biography is represented most extensively in fantastic literature by the twenty-three–volume *Biography of the Life of Manuel* (1904–1929) by James Branch Cabell.

FICTIVE HISTORY. Fiction that implies or reinforces a view of historical reality, or that is itself an imitation of a historical document. As Robert H. Canary observes, all novels are thus in some sense fictive histories, but works of science fiction and fantasy present special problems in that they are frequently laid outside of recognizable historical realities. Such works, however, may constitute fictive histories if they imply a notion of historical process either through Extrapolation* or through employing a widely held historiographical view, such as Historical Cyclism* [46]. See also FUTURE HISTORY; HISTORICAL PLURALITY.

FIRST CONTACT STORY. A science fiction story depicting initial meeting or communication with aliens or extraterrestrials, and a common Subgenre* of science fiction narratives which may take its name from Murray Leinster's story in *Astounding Science Fiction*, "First Contact" (1945).

FIX-UP. Coined by A. E. Van Vogt in his memoirs to describe an extended fictional work comprising stories previously published but altered and connected in the extended text. The term entered the science fiction critical vocabulary through its liberal use in Peter Nicholls' *The Science Fiction Encyclopedia* (1977) [144]. The term seems convenient for a genre that evolved largely in magazines that could accommodate only shorter pieces or Serials,* since the raw material for many novels in the genre has often consisted of ideas previously worked out in short stories. But since the term is widely applied to novels, or books marketed as novels, it has drawn criticism from some authors (notably James Gunn in *Foundation*, no. 30) because of the implied generic distinction between a novel "written" as a novel and one published in segments as shorter pieces. Gunn argues that this suggests the latter are inferior and "episodic," and that "episodic" is itself a deprecatory term. In addition, one might argue that "fix up" from general usage carries a connotation of contrivance and even salvage. A further problem is that the term sometimes confuses manner of publication with manner of composition; novels written as such but excerpted for magazine publication are included under the term as well as groups of short stories reworked to resemble a novel.

FOLK TALE. A tale from oral tradition, as opposed to the literary fairy tale or the *Märchen.** While folk tales often provide the source for such works, they also may be the basis for other fantasy Adaptations* such as horror and ghost stories, as well as a narrative strategy in the works of authors from Ludwig Tieck to Manly Wade Wellman.

FORMULA. "A combination or synthesis of a number of specific cultural conventions with a more universal story form or archetype," according to John G. Cawelti [49]. Cawelti actually refers to two kinds of formulas in this definition: conventional ways of describing people or things, which tend to be specific to particular cultures; and recurrent conventional patterns of story or plot, which tend to be more universal. In the latter sense, "formula" is often confused with genre, particularly in those highly conventionalized forms of popular literature, such as the classical detective story, in which the rules of narrative construction become a key defining factor. However, such a usage becomes especially problematic in fantasy and science fiction, which may draw on narrative formulas from other popular genres and incorporate them into fantastic settings or populate them with fantastic beings (such as the detective story displaced into a science fiction world by Isaac Asimov or the spy thriller displaced into a fantasy world by Katherine Kurtz). While there are a number of narrative formulas specific to both fantasy and science fiction (Frank Cioffi has attempted to identify a number of the latter specific to science fiction of the 1930s [52]), and while both genres certainly partake of the culturally localized stereotypes and conventions identified with formula writing, neither genre can be easily defined according to dominant narrative patterns, at least at the surface level. Some critics, however, notably Mark Rose [160] and Gary K. Wolfe [208], have attempted to identify more broadly thematic formulas for science fiction; in Rose, it is the encounter of human and nonhuman, and in Wolfe the encounter of known and unknown. While neither formula is generative exclusively of science fiction works, each provides a useful means of revealing connections between disparate works both inside and outside the field.

FORTEAN. Of or relating to the works of Charles Fort (1874–1932), an American journalist whose various collections of acounts of unexplained phenomena (*The Book of the Damned*, 1919; *Lo!*, 1931; *Wild Talents*, 1932, etc.) influenced a number of popular science fiction and fantasy writers during the 1930s and 1940s. Though not pretending himself to be a serious theorist, Fort's examples of strange phenomena provided fodder for authors including Eric Frank Russell, Damon Knight, and L. Ron Hubbard.

FREE FANTASY. Fantasy narratives unencumbered by specific ground rules, whether from a source or from the design of the author; the term is C. S. Lewis' [120].

FUNCTION. In the folk or fairy tale, an act performed by a specific character, "defined from the point of view of its significance for the course of the action," according to Vladimir Propp in his classic study *Morphology of the Folktale*, (1928) [155]. Functions are supposedly generative of folktales in a manner analogous to the way in which grammatical functions generate sentences, and thus "serve as stable, constant elements in folktales, independent of who performs them, and how they are fulfilled by the dramatis personae." They also are supposedly finite in number and always occur in the same sequence. Propp identified thirty-one such functions in oral tales; examples are the hero leaving home or magical tests the hero must undergo. Many of Propp's functions remain conventions of modern fantasy narratives, and his techniques of analysis have influenced later structuralist critics and the study of narrative formula in general.

FUTURE HISTORICAL. "A tale of the future using the techniques of the historical novel," according to Isaac Asimov, whose own *Foundation* series (1942–1950) is the most famous example of the type [14].

FUTURE HISTORY. A metafictional device for connecting a number of stories set in a common future, most often associated with the stories published by Robert A. Heinlein during the 1940s (although the chronological charts often associated with future histories had been used as early as 1930 by Olaf Stapledon). Future history chronologies may be either presented by authors in connection with their own stories, as is the case with Heinlein, or derived from an author's work by critics, as is the case with R. D. Mullen's chronology of James Blish's *Cities in Flight* series (1955–1962). Other authors who have employed this common device are Cordwainer Smith, Larry Niven, and Ursula K. Le Guin. See also COSMOGONY; FICTIVE HISTORY; HISTORICAL CYCLISM; HISTORICAL PLURALITY.

FUTURE SHOCK. Journalistic term derived from the title of Alvin Toffler's popular 1970 study of the impact of rapid technological and social change on individuals and the culture at large. The term has been widely invoked in discussions of the value of science fiction, and has arguably had some impact on certain writers in the genre, notably John Brunner. See also FUTUROLOGY.

FUTURE WAR. Although still a common Subgenre* of science fiction, future war tales enjoyed a particular vogue in the latter nineteenth century and were a continuing tradition in Proto Science Fiction.* Used as a generic term, "future war" often refers specifically to such earlier works, sometimes specifically to those produced between the publication of George T. Chesney's *The Battle of Dorking* (1871) and the advent of World War I [56]. Anthologies of more recent science fiction on this theme include Gordon R. Dickson's *Combat SF* (1975) and Reginald Bretnor's three-volume *The Future at War* (1979–1980).

FUTURIANS. A group of science fiction fans from Brooklyn active from 1938 to 1945. "Futurian" is sometimes extended to describe their collective influence on the way science fiction was written—specifically, a shift away from the Superscience* conventions of earlier Pulp* writing and toward a more satirical focus on character and the ways in which individuals might react to technological change. The group included Donald Wollheim, Cyril Kornbluth, Frederik Pohl, Robert Lowndes, James Blish, and Damon Knight, whose *The Futurians* (1977) is a history of the group.

FUTUROLOGY. The interdisciplinary study of possible futures. Coined by German historian Ossip Flechtheim in 1949 but in common use only since the mid–1960s, "futurology" is an attempt to provide a scientific label for the methodical and systematic study of potential future trends and events. Although such movements have been fairly common in the past (a particular outbreak of such thinking in the late 1920s in England is believed by Brian Stableford to have influenced the development of science fiction in that country [22]), their connections to modern science fiction have been relatively slight [81].

G

GADGET SCIENCE FICTION. Almost self-explanatory, but most often associated with science fiction of the Gernsback Era* and the years immediately following. Isaac Asimov suggested this term in 1953 as a means of describing those tales of this period that, in contrast to adventure science fiction, stressed technology at the expense of almost everything else and leaned heavily toward exposition as the brilliant or crusty or mad scientist explained his latest invention in interminable detail to the hero and/or heroine [35]. The term has on occasion been used to refer to more recent science fiction in this tradition, in which the technology appears to be the *raison d'être* of the narrative.

GEDANKENEXPERIMENT. See THOUGHT EXPERIMENT.

GENRE. (French, "type, kind"). Usually, a group of literary works with common defining characteristics or conventions. In its oldest sense, the major historical genres of literature, derived from the Greeks, are drama, epic, and lyric; this led Northrop Frye to speculate that the original principle of generic distinction involved the "radical of presentation," that is, the manner in which a work is conveyed to its audience [92]. In practice, the term has gained much narrower usage and has come to refer to major formal, technical, or even thematic elements that unite groups of works within a larger genre; hence the genre of prose fiction was commonly divided into further genres of novels and romances during the nineteenth century (based on content) or into genres of novels, novellas, and short stories (based on length and the structural conventions governed by length). As a result of the widely varying usages of this term, legitimate debates have arisen concerning whether science fiction and fantasy constitute true genres at all.

Two general approaches to the term "genre" have proved useful in discussing fantastic literature, however. John Cawelti suggested that genres may be identified as "archetype-genres," which relate specific works to broad "universal" forms such as tragedy or romance; or "formula-genres" (more commonly "popular genres") which relate such works to other works with the same specific conventions [49]. A given work of fantasy, then, might be discussed either in terms of other fantasies of the same type, or in terms of the broad tradition of romance to which many fantasies also belong. A second definition, used by Mark Rose, approaches genre not as a means of classification but as a set of reading Protocols,* "a context for writing and reading" [160]. This approach has the advantage of describing how works are written and read in specific times and places, and avoids some of the historical confusion that arises when purely formal definitions of genre are attempted. A problem with many, if not most, definitions of science fiction and fantasy is that they attempt to identify formal characteristics that may seem to connect works that common sense tells us do not readily belong in the same genre. While such formal characteristics may enable historians of science fiction to include, for example, Dante's *Divine Comedy* (1311) as part of the great tradition of Proto Science Fiction,* the contextual approach would correct this by pointing out that neither Dante nor his readers were aware of any science fiction tradition and that modern science fiction readers would not expect to find such a work as the *Divine Comedy* in the pages of their favorite magazines. The term "genre science fiction," as often used by Peter Nicholls and others, generally employs such a contextual approach to genre, and refers to works self-consciously written, published, and received in the context of similar works and acknowledged conventions [144].

Genre is sometimes distinguished from Formula,* which often refers to specific narrative conventions, and "mode," which refers to narrative strategies within a genre (so that, as science fiction evolves toward greater integration with the Mainstream,* it becomes less of a genre unto itself and more of a mode of presentation).

GERNSBACK ERA. Commonly cited as one of the major periods of historical development in twentieth-century science fiction, and specified by Isaac Asimov as the years 1926–1938—or roughly from the founding by Hugo Gernsback of *Amazing Stories* to the beginning of John W. Campbell, Jr.'s editorship of *Astounding Science Fiction* [35]. The dates are of course arguable, since Gernsback began publishing science fiction in his popular technology magazines as early as 1911, and since his own avowed interest in science fiction as a means of popularizing science was never as dominant a force in *Amazing* as Gernsback might have hoped. In any event, the term survives as a general way of describing that period of science fiction in which Gernsback exerted some editorial influence, and perhaps as a way of isolating and defining a body of early science fiction for which few claims of literary or social merit are made.

GHETTO. A kind of literary backwater. Since at least the late 1940s, science fiction writers and editors have complained of the "ghettoization" of the genre by publishers, booksellers, and reviewers. "Ghetto" thus refers not only to the evolution of science fiction as a commercial bookselling category, but to a complex of critical and social attitudes that have come to influence factors as disparate as authors' contracts, book design, the placement of popular reviews, the teaching of the genre, and literary fellowships and awards. While other genre writers have also complained about "ghettoes" of westerns, mysteries, romance novels, and the like, science fiction writers have been perhaps the most vocal and possibly the best-organized group in opposing this tendency.

Anthony Boucher argued that such literary ghettoes arose from four factors: the tendency of popular writers to specialize in a particular genre, the tendency of readers to buy fiction by category, the tendency of academics to increasingly separate popular from "serious" fiction, and the realization on the part of publishers that more predictable sales could be gained by segmenting audiences according to special interests [35]. In fact, the latter factor is arguably the most significant in the historical evolution of the "ghetto" of science fiction, which for much of its history has been dominated by magazines (which have been sold by popular category since the nineteenth century), and which did not enjoy significant paperback publication until long after Robert de Graaf of Pocket Books had discovered the principle of shelving genre books together in order to increase their sales. Similarly, hardbound science fiction did not become widespread until after hardcover publishers had been forced into similar marketing techniques by the success of the "paperback revolution." In more recent years, the very success of science fiction has exacerbated the situation, as authors who have established track records of dependable sales within the genre often find it difficult to persuade publishers to market books in any other way; the most famous examples are Harlan Ellison's *contretemps* with a publisher who attempted to label as science fiction reprints of the author's early realistic and autobiographical writings, and Isaac Asimov's losing argument with a publisher who refused to label his 1972 novel *The Gods Themselves* as science fiction.

GHOST STORY. In the most obvious sense, a supernatural narrative characterized by the presence of spirits of the dead; in a somewhat broader and perhaps more common sense, any narrative that *implies* the presence of such spirits in a significant way, such as Henry James'

"The Turn of the Screw" (1898). In a still broader sense, the term has sometimes been applied to the metaphoric presence of ghosts, as in James Joyce's "The Dead." Julia Briggs includes in her definition stories not only about ghosts, but about "possession and demonic bargains, spirits other than those of the dead, including ghouls, vampires, werewolves, the 'swarths' of living men and the 'ghost-soul' or *Doppelgänger*.*" Such stories, she argues, are "generically related through a common intention of inducing fear by the use of the supernatural," and thus are distinct from the tradition of fantasy which derives from Fairy Tales* and from stories dealing with magical omens or portents [37].

GOLDEN AGE. The earliest and most perfect of the Ages of the World as described by Hesiod in his *Works and Days* (ca. 700 B.C.), and thus often related to Utopian* thinking. In discussions of literary history, however, "golden age" refers to a period of unparalleled productivity and quality in the literary history of a nation or region—such as Latin literature ca. 80 B.C.–14 A.D. In this latter sense, the term is often informally applied to those periods during which popular art forms developed and solidified major conventions and themes; "golden age" has on occasion been defined with only some flippancy as the phase of an individual reader's life during which he or she first fell in love with a genre. In science fiction, however, the term most often refers to the Campbell Era,* and has been even more specifically delimited by Isaac Asimov as the years 1938–1950, during which *Astounding Science Fiction* under Campbell dominated the market and published the early works of a large number of major writers [14]. The term is, as Robert Scholes and Eric Rabkin state, characteristic of science fiction Fandom* in being "overstated, self-approving, and quite uncritical" [178]. However, other Pulp* genres have also been said to have their own golden ages; for example, Sam Lundwall cites the years 1928–1939 for *Weird Tales* magazine, those being the years in which authors such as H. P. Lovecraft, Robert E. Howard, and Clark Ashton Smith published the stories that would eventually come to define their particular Subgenres* [125].

GOTHIC. Originally, relating to Goths, later to Teutonic culture in general, then to "barbarian" cultures, and eventually, in the eighteenth century, to the styles of the Middle Ages [93]. In 1765, Horace Walpole appended the subtitle "A Gothic Tale" to the second edition of his novel *The Castle of Otranto*, and the term quickly entered literary discourse both as a condemnation of works of excessive violence and supernatural extravagance and as a marketing device for a new genre of cheap thrillers. The medieval settings or ruined castles characteristic of many such narratives probably led critics to associate them with the then-despised excesses of Gothic architecture, but the term has survived in literature to describe a variety of ghostly or supernatural tales that have little if anything to do with the devotional meaning of "Gothic" to art historians or the associations with barbarian Europe to historians in general. (Were the latter the case, Sword and Sorcery* would be deserving of the term.) While the Gothic novel as a genre survived well into the nineteenth century, it eventually gave way to genres as disparate as the horror story and the romantic novel (and, according to Brian Aldiss and other critics, science fiction [1]). While horror fiction inherited the more extravagant supernatural appurtenances of the Gothic, the romantic novel, through the Brontës and later Daphne du Maurier, adopted its settings and the conventions surrounding the Gothic villain to spawn a genre of modern popular novels of romantic suspense that have come to appropriate the term *Gothic* for marketing purposes, even though such novels may have little or nothing to do with the supernatural.

GOTHIC HIGH FANTASY. A hybrid Subgenre* combining elements of High Fantasy* and Horror.* Critics Robert H. Boyer and Kenneth J. Zahorski define "Gothic" as supernatural tales concerned with the sense of dread or apprehension upon confronting the unknown or unnatural; in "Gothic high fantasy" these supernatural elements are explainable in terms of the laws of a fully imagined Secondary World,* whereas in "Gothic low fantasy," which is set in the "real world," they are generally not explainable [30].

GOTHIC LOW FANTASY. See GOTHIC HIGH FANTASY.

GOTHIC NOVEL. Originally a historical term used to refer to a genre of popular sensational novels of the late eighteenth and early nineteenth centuries, the term has come to be applied to modern novels using the conventions of that genre, to a broader category of romances featuring exotic settings and often featuring women protagonists, and in some cases to almost any fiction of the supernatural which is heavily atmospheric and not set in a Secondary World.* See GOTHIC; GOTHIC HIGH FANTASY; GOTHIC SCIENCE.

GOTHIC SCIENCE. Scientific or pseudoscientific ideas presented in the framework of Gothic* novels or tales. J. O. Bailey cites as examples alchemy in Edward Bulwer-Lytton's *Zanoni* (1842) and Honore de Balzac's *The Quest of the Absolute* (1834), mesmerism in Edgar Allan Poe's "The Facts in the Case of M. Valdemar" (1845), and chemistry in Nathaniel Hawthorne's "The Birth Mark" (1846) [19]. The phrase has not been widely adopted, but is a convenient term for indicating how in early science fiction–like tales, science was often adapted and altered for atmospheric purposes. The term might also be applied to various attempts at pseudoscientific "explanations" of Gothic conventions, such as Richard Matheson's attempt at a bacterial rationale for vampirism in *I Am Legend* (1954).

GROTESQUE. A style characterized by distorted, warped, or exaggerated representations of reality. Identified as "a branch of the fantastic" by an essay in the *Pall Mall Gazette* in 1888, the term originally referred to the kind of ornamental design originally discovered in excavations of ancient architecture (hence, *Grotteschi* or grottoes). The term gained currency among art historians and was widely used by Horace Walpole, but probably first entered critical discourse through Sir Walter Scott's 1827 *Fortnightly Review* essay "On the Supernatural in Fictitious Composition." From here, apparently, it was picked up by Edgar Allan Poe, who used it in the title of his 1840 collection *Tales of the Grotesque and Arabesque*. While there is some disagreement as to how Poe intended the meaning of these terms—some have argued that his notion of "grotesque" represented the distorted view of reality imposed by human senses and intellect—"grotesque" has since evolved in common usage to refer to distorted or wildly exaggerated representations of reality. It is, as Wolfgang Kayser said in his 1963 study *The Grotesque in Art and Literature*, "the estranged world, our world which has been transformed" [107]. In fantasy, the term is associated, for example, with works such as those of Mervyn Peake, and in the Mainstream* with authors as diverse as Carson McCullers and Günter Grass.

GROUND RULES. Broadly, any rules of causality or physics that are accepted as a given in a work of fiction. While the "ground rules" of realistic fiction are essentially those of the experiential world, works of fantasy contravene these rules and thus, according to Eric Rabkin, become dependent on the internal consistency of their own ground rules [156].

H

HAPPY ENGINEER. "One of the great uninvestigated myths of contemporary science fiction," according to Barry Malzberg, who coined the term to describe the commonly accepted belief that science fiction of the Golden Age* was characterized by technological optimism represented by brilliant engineer-heroes who successfully solved all problems by application of the scientific method. Malzberg argues that the Happy Engineer is a myth associated with John W. Campbell, Jr.'s own beliefs, but not widely reflected in the fiction of his era [129].

HARD SCIENCE FICTION (sometimes also "hardcore science fiction"). Science fiction in which the Ground Rules* are known scientific principles, and in which speculation based on such principles constitutes a significant part of the work. Coined presumably on the model of "hard sciences" (the physical and biological, as opposed to social sciences), "hard science fiction" is ostensibly that "written around known scientific facts or at least not-unproven theories generated by 'real' scientists," according to Norman Spinrad [34]. Thomas N. Scortia somewhat more narrowly defines it as a "closely reasoned technological story" [36]. Neither definition quite encompasses the breadth with which the term is actually used, however. In some cases it refers only to stories in which the setting is carefully worked out from known scientific principles (as in the work of Hal Clement or Larry Niven), in other cases to stories in which the plot hangs on such a principle, and in still other cases to almost any science fiction associated with such stories in time or place. In the last sense, the term may become almost synonymous with science fiction of the Campbell Era.* See also SOFT SCIENCE FICTION.

HEGEMONIC NOVUM. According to Darko Suvin, the "Novum,"* or "strange newness," which is at the center of science fiction narratives is "hegemonic" in that it "determines the whole narrative logic" of the tale. Some other critics and reviewers have adopted "hegemonic novum" as a concise, if somewhat eccentric, way of characterizing science fiction [187].

HEROIC FANTASY. Often commercially applied to Sword and Sorcery* tales featuring muscular barbarian heroes, but sometimes to any variety of Epic* or Quest* fantasy, particularly those that derive from specific heroic traditions, such as Arthurian tales.

HERO TALE. A variety of Folk Tale* dealing with the adventures of a local or traditional hero; sometimes cited as the precursor in folklore of Heroic Fantasy.*

HETEROTOPIA. Originally a medical and biological term referring to a displacement of an organ or an organism; thus, broadly, a "displacement." "Heterotopia" was suggested by Robert Plank in 1968 as a convenient term for works of fiction that invent "not only characters but also settings." Plank included science fiction, much fantasy, and utopian fiction under this term, which in this sense is obviously derivative of Utopia* [151]. Although not widely adopted, the term was invoked in the subtitle of Samuel R. Delany's novel *Triton* (1976): "An Ambiguous Heterotopia."

HIEROPHANY. Mircea Eliade's term for any specific object or being in which is manifest the numinous and sacred, from "elementary hierophanies" of stones and trees to the "supreme hierophany" of the incarnation of God. Any hierophany is also a "kratophany," or manifestation of power [79]. See also NUMINA.

HIGH FANTASY. Fantasy set in a fully imagined Secondary World,* according to Boyer and Zahorski, as opposed to Low Fantasy* which concerns supernatural intrusions into the "real" world [31].

HISTORICAL CYCLISM. The tendency of many science fiction narratives to adopt one of several cyclic views of history, perhaps most frequently those of Arnold Toynbee or Oswald Spengler. The term has been used by Paul Carter [48] and others, although the more specific "Spenglerian" has sometimes been invoked to describe works by those writers, such as James Blish or A. E. Van Vogt, who deliberately adapted Spengler's notions of historical periodicity in fictional contexts. Carter suggests that the dominance of periodicity in the natural sciences may have made a parallel view of history attractive to many science fiction writers; it is equally possible, however, that cyclic history is merely one of a limited number of ways of imagining the future and that it inevitably became a major theme in science fiction by virtue of the limited alternatives. A great many of the Future Histories* of science fiction, and certainly Donald Wollheim's "consensus Cosmogony,"* adopted a limited cyclic view of future history, with one or two periods of reversion and catastrophe followed by an eventual millenium or Utopia.*

HISTORICAL PLURALITY. Multiplicity of historical meanings or theories embodied in fiction. Samuel R. Delany has suggested that, in addition to the Theoretical Plurality* by which science fiction of the 1930s and 1940s challenged the hegemony of accepted scientific tenets and limitations, the genre developed a "historical plurality" through which it examined and challenged various notions of historical development, often within the same series of stories. Isaac Asimov's "Foundation" series (1942–1951) is cited as an example [71]

HORROR. A genre of popular fiction unusual in that it is labeled not according to its own conventions or structures, but according to its desired effect. This leads to some difficulties in attempting to draw generic lines between horror and fantasy or horror and science fiction (John W. Campbell, Jr.'s story "Who Goes There," for example, might properly be described as a science fiction horror story), although a number of critics have made the attempt. Roger C. Schlobin has argued that horror is virtually the opposite of fantasy, with the former presenting a maimed and destructive notion of the natural world threatening the protagonists and by extension the reader, whereas fantasy offers the promise of greater worlds beyond and is hopeful where horror is pessimistic [169]. Although horror has seldom been clearly defined as a genre beyond its evocation of fear and dread, it has come to be a widely accepted book-marketing category, and most, if not all, works so marketed contain supernatural elements.

HOUSEHOLD TALE. Jakob and Wilhelm Grimm's term for their story collections which eventually became universally known as Fairy Tales.* The term probably refers to the manner in which the tales were transmitted through oral tradition, both by parents telling them to their children and by household workers telling them as entertainment during boring or repetitive tasks.

HUGO AWARD. The Science Fiction Achievement Award, presented annually since 1953 (except for 1954) by the World Science Fiction conventions and voted on by fans who are members of those conventions.

HUMAN RACISM. Term used by C. S. Lewis (*The Abolition of Man*, 1945) to attack the ideas of Scientism* which he perceived in the novels of H. G. Wells and others. Lewis strongly objected to the proposition that humans enjoyed a kind of manifest destiny to conquer the universe, and argued against it in his novels as well as his criticism. The implied Cosmogony* of science fiction derived by Donald A. Wollheim is a good example of the sort of notion that offended Lewis.

HYPOTHETICAL PROBABILITY. "What would be probable if the initial situation occurred"; C. S. Lewis' term to describe the Ground Rules* of narratives based on unrealistic or fantastic presuppositions [120].

I

ICONOGRAPHY. Originally from art history, where it was used to discuss the icons of early art and later (ca. 1900) to discuss the significance of images or patterns of images in works of art. "Iconography" has occasionally been invoked as a method of examining popular genres through their recurrent patterns of imagery. Gary K. Wolfe has termed such images in science fiction and fantasy "icons," and defined these as "something we are willing to accept because of our familiarity with the genre" but which may retain their power even when isolated from specific fictional contexts, as opposed to stereotypes, which originate in the culture at large, or conventions, which are specific to groups of texts. Examples in science fiction are robots, cities, monsters, and spacecraft [208].

ICONOLOGY. Sometimes used interchangeably with Iconography,* although some critics of art (notably Erwin Panofsky) have argued that iconology more properly refers to the use of visual images to examine a more general history of culture or ideas. The term has been used in the study of fantastic literature by Theodore Ziolkowski, who used it as a method of tracing the rise of materialism in fiction through several key fantastic images, such as the mirror, as represented in various works of fiction over time [216].

IDEA AS HERO. Kingsley Amis' characterization of much early science fiction. Edmund Crispin once suggested a type of detective story which he characterized with the term "plot as hero," and on this model Amis suggested a parallel type of science fiction which he called "idea as hero." The primacy of the central idea, he suggested, tended to make the story effective in paraphrase (and hence perhaps to generate word-of-mouth transmission which was of importance especially during the Pulp* era), but de-emphasized both character and style, and in some cases even plot [8]. See also LITERATURE OF IDEAS; THOUGHT-VARIANT.

IDIOT PLOT. Probably coined by James Blish, but popularized through the reviews of Damon Knight, who defined it as a plot that "is kept in motion solely by virtue of the fact that everybody involved is an idiot." Specifically, he refers to stories in which characters act at the convenience of the author rather than through any perceivable motivation, and uses the term to attack fantastic works that seem based on the assumption that fantastic elements obviate the need for fictional credibility. Similar terms have been employed by other critics of popular fiction and film [110].

IMAGINARY VOYAGE. In its broadest sense, any account of a voyage that did not actually take place, whether or not fantastic elements are present, as long as the voyage constitutes a central part of the narrative. Philip Babcock Gove persuasively demonstrated that the imaginary voyage constituted a major genre of imaginative fiction from the sixteenth century to the present, but had some difficulty in arriving at any sort of a consensus definition of the genre. The earliest definition, by A. J. Tieje, specified that such voyages should be aimed at either literary criticism, at "amusement through the introduction of the wildly fantastic," or at social improvement, and that they should take the reader into "unexplored regions." Later definitions specified that the lands visited should be little known or imaginary, that the function of the tale should be satirical, or that a description of the society found at the end of the voyage should be central. Almost certainly a literary outgrowth of the traveller's tale, the imaginary voyage is of considerable importance in the history of fantastic literature because of its early treatment of extraterrestrial, subterranean, or "lost" civilizations [95]. See also VOYAGES EXTRAORDINAIRES.

IMAGINATION. Term used by Coleridge, MacDonald, and others to describe a higher faculty than mere Fancy.* See also FANCY.

IMAGINATIVE FANTASY. C. N. Manlove's category of those fantasies that seek to establish a fully realized fantastic world, as opposed to those that merely whimsically build closed systems [132]. In a later essay [171] Manlove omitted this distinction between "imaginative" and "fanciful" fantasy. See also FANCY.

IMAGINATIVE FICTION. An early attempt at defining a Supergenre* that would include both fantasy and science fiction. While some might find the term redundant, L. Sprague de Camp defined it as modern stories that are "nonrealistic, imaginative, based upon assumptions contrary to everyday experience, often highly fanciful and often laid in settings remote in time and space from those of everyday life" [35]. See also FANTASTIC ROMANCE.

IMPOSSIBLE. Perhaps the most frequently cited defining characteristic of fantasy. Such definitions often note that fantasy deals with the impossible, as opposed, say, to science fiction, which deals with what might be possible given the conditions of the universe as described to us by science. The term is somewhat value-laden in that notions of what is possible, and therefore of what is impossible, vary from culture to culture and from age to age—even to some extent from individual to individual. Neither psychotic constructs on the one hand nor religious texts on the other are usually regarded as belonging to the fantasy genre, though each may describe impossible events or beings.

INKLINGS. A group of writers and scholars who met informally on Thursday evenings at Oxford from the early 1930s until 1949; since the membership of the group prominently included C. S. Lewis, J. R. R. Tolkien, and Charles Williams, and since occasionally members would read aloud from works in progress, the term has come to refer to the "school" of Christian Fantasy* writing that derived from the mutual influence of members of this group upon each other. Humphrey Carpenter's *The Inklings* (1978) is a history of the group. See also OXFORD CHRISTIANS.

INNER SPACE. J. G. Ballard's term for a group of biological and psychological themes which he viewed as more appropriate to modern science fiction than the focus on "outer space" and technology that had earlier characterized the genre. Writing in the May 1962 issue of the British magazine *New Worlds*, Ballard called for more "psycho-literary ideas, more meta-biological and meta-chemical concepts, private time systems, synthetic psychologies and space-times, more of the remote, somber half-worlds one glimpses in the paintings of schizophrenics, all in all a complete speculative poetry and fantasy of science" ("Which Way to Inner Space?" *New Worlds* 40 [May 1962]: 117–118). The term came widely to be associated with the New Wave,* not only in terms of its themes, but in terms of the styles and narrative structures used to accommodate such themes.

INSTRUMENTALIZATION. Means by which the devices of fantasy may be appropriated for specific social or cultural ends, usually by the dominant culture and usually by recasting fantastic narratives to reflect chosen values [217].

INTERNATIONAL ASSOCIATION FOR THE FANTASTIC IN THE ARTS. Academic organization that promotes the study of all aspects of the fantastic in a variety of disciplines, primarily through its annual conference. The organization was founded in 1982 as an outgrowth of the International Conference on the Fantastic in the Arts, which began in 1980.

INTERPLANETARY ROMANCE. Broadly, an adventure tale set on another, usually primitive, planet. Largely under the influence of Edgar Rice Burroughs, American science fiction from World War I until the founding of *Amazing Stories* in 1926 was characterized by action-filled narratives set in exotic locations, including the moon and other planets. Although often referred to at the time as Scientific Romances,* these works, which seldom focused on the technology of travel to other planets, have come increasingly to be referred to as "interplanetary romances," perhaps in part to distinguish them from the scientific romances of H. G. Wells. Besides Burroughs, the major authors in this Subgenre* included Otis Adelbert Kline, Ralph Milne Farley, and Homer Eon Flint, although on occasion the term has been more broadly used to include such otherworldly fictions as those of C. S. Lewis. See also SCIENCE FANTASY; SWORD AND SORCERY.

INVASION NOVEL. A type of novel, popular in England during the last quarter of the nineteenth century, which depicted invasions of England by external aggressors (usually from Europe, but occasionally from the Orient). The prototype may well have been Sir George Chesney's *The Battle of Dorking* (1871), and among the best of the type is Erskine Childers' *The Riddle of the Sands* (1903). H. G. Wells' *The War of the Worlds* (1898) almost certainly owes something to this tradition, which was effectively parodied by P. G. Wodehouse in *The Swoop! Or How Clarence Saved England* (1909). See also FUTURE WAR.

INVENTION. In its original rhetorical sense, the discovery of material as the first step in argument or oration. H. G. Wells, however, used this term for the hypothetical initial situation upon which the fantastic events in a narrative are founded [150]. See also HYPOTHETICAL PROBABILITY.

IRRATIONALISM. A world view that holds that the universe and humanity are not governed by any fundamental principles of reason. W. Warren Wagar cites Friedrich Nietzsche, Sigmund Freud, and Jean-Paul Sartre as major exponents of this tradition, which finds expression in fantastic literature through works as various of those of Franz Kafka and the New Wave* in science fiction [198]. In a considerably more technical sense, L. Sprague de Camp uses the term to describe a technique in humorous writing in which a character is made to behave in a deliberately stupid or irrational way to achieve comic effects and provide the reader with a sense of superiority [84]. See also ABSURD.

IRRATIONALITY. See IRRATIONALISM (de Camp usage).

ISLAND UTOPIA. A work portraying a utopian or satirical utopian community isolated from the world by virtue of its being located on an undiscovered or hidden island. Before extraterrestrial or subterranean voyages became accepted conventions in fantastic literature, this was perhaps the most common means of accounting for a society's isolation in a work of fiction [8].

ISOLATED SYSTEM. See SYSTEMS MODEL.

J

JOY. The dominant emotion associated with the Eucatastrophe* in J. R. R. Tolkien's discussion of fairy tales. "Joy" is essentially for Tolkien a religious concept, and one that implies the promise of salvation in the happy endings of such stories [194]. For C. S. Lewis, who also adopted the term, it came to represent a kind of "signpost" leading to the discovery of faith—again, the promise of salvation but not the salvation itself [121].

JUNIOR NOVEL. See JUVENILE.

JUVENILE. Term favored by publishers and librarians (along with "junior novel" and "young adult") to characterize works written for the teenage market. In this sense, the term usually means books that are somewhat longer and more sophisticated than children's books, although often the term is used to include any book written for children. A great many science fiction and fantasy authors have written for this market, and some, such as Lloyd Alexander, have gained considerable reputations in the genre at large through such works (although in general, fantasy juveniles are less segregated from the adult market than are science fiction juveniles). The science fiction juvenile as a definable market probably began in 1947 with the publication of Robert A. Heinlein's *Rocket Ship Galileo*; Heinlein followed this with a series of novels published by Scribner's, and the John C. Winston Company further exploited the market with a series beginning in 1952 that included works by Lester del Rey, Chad Oliver, Arthur C. Clarke, Poul Anderson. While a number of major writers have written whole series specifically for the juvenile market, others, such as del Rey, have argued that the segregation of specific works into such a market is artificial [74], and indeed a number of so-called juveniles were either written as standard science fiction novels or later released as such.

K

KAKOTOPIA. Term used rather eccentrically by Lewis Mumford (*The Pentagon of Power*, 1970) to refer to a concept more usually labeled Dystopia.*.

KINEMATIC. A narrative technique identified by Algis Budrys that borrows from film the devices of rapid motion, sensory stimulation, and "compressed data" in so that the prose "engages some of the information-processing habits the reader has developed from watching movies and TV" [42]. Such techniques are of course widely used by authors of popular fiction in a variety of genres; an example in science fiction might be Gregory Benford's *Artifact* (1985).

KITCHEN-SINK STORY. Damon Knight's term for a story overwhelmed by the inclusion of almost any new idea that may occur to the author in the process of writing it; some such uncontrolled stories may be found as the most extreme examples of the Thought-Variant* stories of the 1930s [110].

KRATOPHANY. See HIEROPHANY.

KUNSTMÄRCHEN. The "art fairy tale"; used by early nineteenth-century German romantic writers to distinguish their works from the traditional Märchen.*

KUNSTSAGE. Sometimes used by the German romantics to describe stories written in imitation of legends or family histories.

L

LABOR DAY GROUP. Coined by Thomas M. Disch to describe a group of science fiction writers born between 1945 and 1948 and who began publishing between 1969 and 1973. Disch labeled such writers the "Labor Day Group" because of their regular attendance at World Science Fiction conventions, traditionally held over the Labor Day weekend and regarded as the major event in science fiction Fandom.* Disch argued that this group of writers, which includes George R. R. Martin, Vonda McIntyre, Ed Bryant, and John Varley, was influenced by the expectations of the fan community to the detriment of their own personal visions, and cites—perhaps somewhat circularly—the frequent awards won by these writers from the fans as evidence of such involvement [75]. Martin's rebuttal to Disch's charges appeared in the December 1981 issue of *The Magazine of Fantasy and Science Fiction.*

LAWS OF ROBOTICS. Widely adopted rules governing the behavior of science fiction robots. A critical term only in that it has generated a degree of controversy, the three famous "laws of robotics" derived by Isaac Asimov and John W. Campbell, Jr., following the publication of Asimov's first two robot stories in 1941 (and first formulated in his "Liar!" *Astounding Science Fiction*, May 1941) are in actuality narrative rules convenient for generating later "puzzle" stories about robots. The laws state that a robot must not harm or allow harm to come to a human being, a robot must obey orders given by humans unless they conflict with the first law, and a robot must protect its own existence as long as this does not conflict with the first two laws.

LEGEND. In its folkloric sense, a short narrative associated either with a historical individual or a particular landscape. Some scholars distinguish between "local legends" fixed in one locality and "migratory legends," which are transmitted from place to place and adapted to local conditions. More broadly, the term has come to mean any narrative passed down through oral tradition, often distinguished from Myth* by its stronger basis in historical events. While some specific legends, such as those of Arthur, have had particularly strong thematic influences on fantasy narratives, the general tone or style of legends has been even more widely adopted in both fantasy and science fiction, by authors ranging from Lord Dunsany to Cordwainer Smith.

LITERARY ECOLOGY. See ECOLOGY.

LITERATURE OF IDEAS. Along with Sense of Wonder* and Modern Mythology,* one of the most common popular descriptions of the appeal of science fiction. Used in the 1950s by James Blish and Isaac Asimov, the phrase has been traced by Samuel R. Delany as far back as Balzac [72], although it is doubtful that the science fiction usage of the term is directly connected to such earlier usages. The argument implied by the term is that science fiction traffics in intellectual constructs rather than in character, style, or narrative complexity, but inconsistent usage renders the term of limited use. On the one hand, it can hardly be seriously claimed that Mainstream Fiction* cannot support ideas, while on the other trivial notions or frivolous conceits may often pass for the "ideas" of science fiction. (See Thought-Variant.*) The term nevertheless is important in signifying a common definition of science fiction most often associated with Hard Science Fiction.* See also IDEA AS HERO.

LOGICAL FANTASY. T. E. Apter's term for fantasy concerned with the set of logical structures by which we come to understand the world. Jorge Luis Borges, for example, attacks the notion of logic itself by using it to construct fantastic or absurd situations [11]. The term has also occasionally been used to refer to the rigorously worked out fantasies characteristic of John W. Campbell, Jr.'s magazine *Unknown*, for which Campbell demanded that rules of magic be obeyed as logically and systematically as rules of science in science fiction.

LOGIC OF CHARACTER. See LOGIC OF PREMISE.

LOGIC OF PREMISE. H. G. Wells' notion that in a given fantastic narrative the reader should be asked to assume only a single basic premise or Invention* [203]. Jack Williamson has characterized this as "logic of premise" and cited it—along with "logic of character"—as one of the two central principles of successful fantasy writing [84]. See also HYPOTHETICAL PROBABILITY.

LOST RACE FANTASY. A Subgenre* of the fantastic especially popular during the latter part of the nineteenth century and which in its early expressions, according to Thomas P. Clareson, was largely a modification of Utopia.* These narratives of the discovery of hidden or forgotten civilizations are sometimes claimed for the history of science fiction as well as for fantasy [53].

LOW FANTASY. Narratives in which the fantastic element intrudes on the "real world," as opposed to fantasies set all or partially in a Secondary World,* according to Robert H. Boyer and Kenneth J. Zahorski [31]. See also HIGH FANTASY.

LUDDISM. A popular movement in England from 1811 to 1816 in which masked bands of men attempted to destroy machines associated primarily with the textile industry. The name comes from Ned Lud, who was said to have broken into a house in 1779 and destroyed two knitting machines. Popularized by C. P. Snow in his 1959 *The Two Cultures and the Scientific Revolution*, the term has come to refer to almost any antiscientific or antitechnological bias. While this meaning has been retained in defenses of science fiction as bridging the Two Cultures,* Luddism (or its variant, "neo-luddism") is also sometimes used to refer to antiscientific attitudes in fictional, often Post-Holocaust,* societies such as that in Leigh Brackett's *The Long Tomorrow* (1955).

M

MAGICAL FANTASY. Used by Jane Mobley as an alternative term to High Fantasy,* but with the added implication of fantasy that serves a shamanistic or ritual-like function; opposed to Supernatural Fiction* [135].

MAGIC REALISM (sometimes also "Magical Realism"). A style and narrative technique combining realism with elements of the fantastic, either through vivid language and metaphors or through the introduction of fantastic events into the narrative itself. Such narratives may also partake of aspects of oral tradition and Legend.* The term is most often applied to Latin American writers, among whom it has become a recognizable tradition (the most famous example perhaps being Gabriel Garcia Marquez's *Cien Anōs de Soledad* (1967; trans. 1970 as *One Hundred Years of Solitude*), although authors of other nationalities, such as Peter Carey in Australia, have also been related to this tradition.

MAGIC TIME. See SACRED TIME.

MAINSTREAM FICTION. Fiction that is not written, published, marketed, or reviewed as part of a popular genre. The term may have gained currency during the ascendancy of the Pulp* magazines to distinguish those magazines directed at a general audience from those directed at special-interest audiences; in any event, it has since been adopted by publishers as a rather vague category for marketing or displaying books in bookstores. Sometimes it refers to all nongenre fiction, from literary classics to ephemeral bestsellers, and sometimes it refers more specifically to "Mid-List"* authors whose works are neither heavily promoted nor directed at a genre audience. Among science fiction and fantasy writers and critics, "mainstream" is even more loosely employed to refer to almost anything that is not science fiction or fantasy, and "mainstream author" to refer to any author whose major work or reputation lies outside the field. Such references are often acompanied by complaints—often justified—that such works and authors are granted a frequently undeserved mantle of respectability denied to genre authors; this situation is not helped by publishers who often seek to broaden the market for a book by denying its genre (thus, the ironic complaint that a sure way to tell if a book by a mainstream author is science fiction is if the dust jacket proclaims it *not* to be science fiction).

An early example of the usage of this term within the science fiction community may be found in a letter from Isaac Asimov to the *Bulletin of the Atomic Scientists* (13, May 1957), in which he argued that much science fiction was as well written as "many 'mainstream' novels." An example of the rhetorical misuse of the term which has since become common in science fiction Fandom* is Donald A. Wollheim's astonishing reference to "*Portnoy's Complaint, The Love Machine, The Arrangement*, and the rest of that constant stream of psychiatrists' couch and bedroom agonies that mark the triumphs of the mainstream" [212]. Usages such as this led critic George Turner to describe "mainstream" as a "term of insolence" and complain that "sf is the only genre which ever had the blazing impudence to announce itself worthy of a consideration separate from and beyond the body of traditional (whatever they thought that word meant) literature" [196]. An anthology by Harry Harrison (*The Light Fantastic: Science Fiction Classics from the Mainstream*, 1971) contains a useful introductory essay by James Blish on these issues [28].

There is some confusion resulting from the more common use of this term to refer to the dominant traditions of an art form or genre, or the use common in jazz parlance since the 1950s to refer to jazz which has its roots in a particular historical period, that is, the swing era. In the latter sense, "mainstream science fiction" is sometimes used to refer to Modern Science Fiction.*

MÄRCHEN. German term loosely translated as "Fairy Tale"* or "Folk Tale,"* although neither is precise; in its original meaning from the middle high German *Mare*, it meant news or gossip. The traditional oral tales collected by the Grimms and others are sometimes referred to as *Volksmärchen*, or folk tales, to distinguish them from the Kunstmärchen, or literary imitations such as were written by Ludwig Tieck, Novalis, and others.

MARVELOUS. "The supernatural accepted"; Todorov's term to distinguish works in which the supernatural is accepted as a given (the marvelous) from those in which it is explained (the Uncanny*) [193].

MASTER IDEAS. Algis Budrys' characterization of several themes that became dominant during science fiction's Golden Age.* Budrys identified several "master ideas" deriving from Superscience* themes of the 1930s which established themselves as staples of Modern Science Fiction.* Such ideas, he argued, should not be confused with the specific scientific or technological themes used to explore them; examples are the loss of identity, the "white man's burden" (concerning the responsibilities inherent in advanced society or technology), the by-products of technological advance, and the failure of technological dictatorships through technology itself [43].

MATERIAL FANTASY. (Russian, *material 'naja fantasticnost'*). Term borrowed from Dostoevsky to describe the fantastic in authors such as Edgar Allan Poe as distinct from the "unknowable" horrors of earlier Gothic writers. According to Julius Kagarlitski, the achievement of Jules Verne was to interpret the traditions of material fantasy in a directly realistic spirit, giving rise to Realistic Fantasy* as a precursor of modern science fiction [54]. The term has been used in a slightly different sense by John Cawelti, for whom it meant a fantasy "in which the writer imagines a world materially different from ordinary reality, but in which the characters and the situations they confront are still governed by the general truths of human experience." Cawelti distinguished this from "Moral Fantasy,"* which represents a more idealized version of our own world, as in nonfantastic popular genres [49].

MATTER. Any one of three broad categories of subject matter for the medieval romance, identified by the thirteenth-century poet Jean Bodel, and which have since become traditionally known as the "matters" of France, Rome, and Britain. The matter of Britain included much Arthurian material that has since provided inspiration for innumerable fantasies.

MECHANISTIC. Sometimes applied to fantastic literature in its original sense of the Aristotelian doctrine of efficient causes, and sometimes in the sense of early Cosmologies.* The term has also been given a specific usage by Arthur C. Clarke in distinguishing two types of space-travel fiction: the "mechanistic," in which space is traversed through technological means, and the "nonmechanistic," in which it is traversed through psychic forces, dreams, visions, or supernatural intervention [35].

MEDICAL UTOPIA. Suggested by Ernest Bloch (*The Principle of Hope*, 1959) for "Golden Age"* Utopias* characterized by long life or immortality, freedom from disease, and eternal youth [187].

MEDIEVAL FUTURISM. John Carnell's term for science fiction stories set in a future, often Post-Holocaust,* environment in which medieval history provides all or part of the model for the imagined social structure [125]. See also POSTHISTORY.

MENIPPEA. A tradition of classical satire that, according to Mikhail Bakhtin, prefigured much modern fantastic literature in its violation of the norms of realism and its fluidity of structure; examples include Apuleius' *The Golden Ass* and Lucian's *Strange Story*. Rosemary Jackson borrowed the term to discuss essential qualities of fantastic texts [106]. See also ANATOMY.

METAFICTION. Generally, fiction that takes as its primary subject matter the nature of fiction itself or the fictional process. Suggested by William Gass, the term has been widely appropriated by European and American critics to describe works that incorporate the processes of criticism or that depend upon their own discourse as the only verifiable fictional world. Thus, qualities of narrative voice, formal structure, philosophical speculation, and genre may play significant roles in such fiction. While Robert Scholes has incorporated the concept of metafiction into his ideas of Fabulation* (defining metafiction as "experimental fabulation" [174]), the term has been widely used in other contexts as well. In science fiction and fantasy, it is often associated with the New Wave* and with such authors as Samuel R. Delany, J. G. Ballard, and Peter Beagle.

METAMORPHOSIS. A fantasy narrative based on "impossible personal change," according to W. R. Irwin, such as the transformation of a human into a beast or an insect [105].

METAPHYSICAL. Apart from the traditional literary historical meaning of this term, it has been applied specifically to the genres of myth, Folk Tale,* and fantasy by Darko Suvin, who observes that in such genres physics is related to ethics; by denying the "autonomy" of a neutral physics such genres become "metaphysical" [187].

METAPHYSICAL FICTION. Edward Bulwer-Lytton's term for narratives, such as his own *A Strange Story* (1861), in which "typical" (as opposed to allegorical) characters are thrown into often-fantastic situations in order to explore philosophical or "metaphysical" ideas [127].

MICROCOSMIC ROMANCE. Subgenre* popularized during the 1920s especially by Ray Cummings, whose *The Girl in the Golden Atom* (1919) described adventures in a world-within-world of submicroscopic size. Although the idea had been present in nineteenth-century science fiction, it was largely because of Cummings that it became a staple of the Pulp* era, surviving well into the 1930s and recurring in various forms even later [22].

MIDDLE LANDSCAPE. One of the key myths of modern Western cultural history, according to Leo Marx and other cultural historians. The "middle landscape" lies somewhere between the pastoral and the technological and exhibits the tensions and tendencies of each. Elizabeth Cummins Cogell has argued that this myth survives and has to some extent been reclaimed for an urban society by science fiction works which combine it with Apocalyptic* themes [59].

MID-LIST. Publishing term, used imprecisely to refer to authors whose works, though possibly enjoying a steady rate of sale, fall somewhere between specific generic markets and highly promoted Bestsellers.* See also MAINSTREAM FICTION.

MILLENIALISM. (also "millenarianism"). Derived from the Christian prophecy of the return to earth of Christ after 1,000 years, and widely used to describe any belief in a cataclysmic or salvationary end to the existing social, economic, or political order with its attendant problems. While some social historians have perceived millenialist tendencies in the popularity of science fiction or fantastic literature in general, the term is more often used in reference to specific themes or motives in the fiction itself. See, for example, COSMIC DISASTER STORY; DESIRE; ESCHATOLOGICAL ROMANCE.

MIMESIS. Literally, "imitation." Apart from its traditional meanings associated with representational or nonfantastic literature, and specific thematic meanings associated with the science fiction theme of the imitation of one life form by another, "mimesis" has been suggested by Alberto Manguel as a specific technique characteristic of much fantasy, namely, the technique whereby "seemingly unrelated acts . . . secretly dramatize each other" [130]. Portents in nature of dramatic events are an example of the technique, which like a number of similar techniques suggests an ethical physics for the imagined world. See also CONDITIONAL JOY; METAPHYSICAL.

MIRRORSHADE SCHOOL. See CYBERPUNK.

MODE. In general usage, a fashion or convention; in literary usage, a convention or group of conventions that characterize a type of literature. Northrop Frye distinguishes five modes in literature—myth, romance, high mimetic, low mimetic, and ironic—and associates them with the powers assumed by the protagonist toward the people and environment around him [92]. Largely because of Frye's formulation, a number of critics, among them Rosemary Jackson [106] and Kathryn Hume [102], have explored the notion that fantastic literature may be more properly regarded as a mode than as a genre.

MODERN FANTASY. Most commonly used to describe the contemporary genre of popular literary fantasy, and to distinguish it both from related genres such as science fiction and from antecedents such as the Romance* or the Fairy Tale.* Although fantasy as a commercial market category is largely the product of the immense popularity of J. R. R. Tolkien's *Lord of the Rings* during the 1960s, critics usually trace the beginning of modern fantasy to Victorian England. A common work cited as a somewhat arbitrary starting date for the genre is George MacDonald's 1858 *Phantastes*, although some writers have placed the beginnings of a self-conscious genre as late as 1894 with William Morris' *The Wood beyond the World* or as early as 1837 with Sara Coleridge's *Phantasmion*.

MODERN MYTHOLOGY. Very loosely used catch-phrase to describe modern fantastic literature in general and science fiction in particular; the argument is essentially that such fiction serves for a technological age the role served by Myth* in earlier societies. See also NEW MYTHOLOGY.

MODERN SCIENCE FICTION. Commonly used to refer to science fiction published primarily in *Astounding Science Fiction* following John W. Campbell, Jr.'s assuming the editorship of that magazine in 1937, although Donald A. Wollheim defines it as science fiction published after Isaac Asimov's *Foundation* series (1942–1949) [212]. As Algis Budrys points out, the term probably gained currency after its use in the 1946 anthology *Adventures in Time and Space*, edited by Raymond J. Healy and J. Francis McComas, who used it to differentiate the predominantly *Astounding* stories in that collection from earlier traditions of science fiction. Budrys (who capitalizes the term "Modern Science Fiction" to distinguish it from general references to modern works in the genre) further suggests that the period ends about 1950 and is followed by Post-Modern Science Fiction* [43].

MONOMYTH. Joseph Campbell's term, borrowed from James Joyce's *Finnegans Wake*, to describe the primordial hero myth of separation, initiation, and return. The term has been widely appropriated by critics of fantasy [45].

MORAL FANTASY. John Cawelti's term for popular fictions in which the narrative world is exaggerated or idealized according to fantasies of wish-fulfillment or nostalgia, as opposed to works of Material Fantasy* [49].

MOTIF. Recurrent or signal narrative events or figures, especially in folklore, where thousands of motifs and variants have been identified—many of them equally common in fantasy narratives. Science fiction has evolved a complex set of motifs of its own, and for a number of years various scholars have proposed a motif-index to the literature, presumably on the model of Stith Thompson's *Motif-Index of Folk-Literature* (1955–1958). No one has yet completed such an index, nor has anyone quite explained what it would be for.

MUNDANE. Originally from Fandom,* where it is used as either a noun or an adjective to describe people or concerns either outside the science fiction community or outside science-fictional worlds. The term early entered science fiction discourse as shorthand for fiction set in the "real" world. While this led to C. M. Kornbluth's rather improbably describing Cervantes' *Don Quixote* as "a mundane tale about a lunatic" [67], it has nevertheless gained currency in the work of critics of the genre such as Samuel R. Delany.

MYTH. Employed with abandon by scholars of every sort of fantastic literature, and among the most redefined and debated of all cultural concepts. While most scholars have abandoned the nineteenth-century view of myth as a marvelous story associated with something called the "primitive mind," more recent definitions have ranged from any narrative associated with a rite (Lord Raglan) to "the expression of unobservable realities" (H. W. Bartsch) to a tale designed to give meaning and structure to life by providing models for behavior (Mircea Eliade) to an instrument of language designed to provide logical resolutions for contradictions within a culture (Claude Levi-Strauss). Myth may be taken to mean a "sacred" narrative, an explanatory cosmological tale, a means of bestowing or transmitting values, or even, in the Jungian sense, as evidence of a general racial unconscious. As a narrative mode, the term's use in literary criticism has perhaps most been influenced by Northrop Frye, who defined it simply as a stylized narrative featuring superhuman beings whose actions could "happen only in stories" [92]. A discussion of science fiction and fantasy in the context of particular myth patterns is Casey Fredericks' *The Future of Eternity* [89]. See also MONOMYTH; NEW MYTHOLOGY.

MYTH FANTASY. Fantasy Adaptations* whose source materials are pre-existing bodies of mythology; used as a category by anthologists Robert Boyer and Kenneth Zahorski [31] and by bibliographer Diana Waggoner [199]. Examples might be the work of novelists such as Thomas Burnett Swann or Robert Holdstock.

MYTHIC DISPLACEMENT. See DISPLACEMENT.

MYTHIC TIME. See SACRED TIME.

MYTHOLATRY. Presumably a portmanteau of "myth" and "idolatry," and used disparagingly by James Blish in describing the work of writers, mostly in the New Wave,* who questioned or attacked the rationalistic world view of earlier science fiction [16]. See also ANTISCIENTISM; SCIENCE FANTASY.

MYTHOLOGICAL TALE. One of a group of tales "whose norms are supposed to have subtemporally (timelessly or continuously) determined man's basic relations to man and nature," according to Darko Suvin, the mythological tale differs from other forms of fantasy and folklore in that it forms a systematic whole with others of its type [187].

MYTHOMORPHIC. Fiction in the shape of myth; fiction that is structurally or morphologically similar to tales from mythology.

MYTHOPOEIA, MYTHOPOEIC. Conscious artistic fabrication of myths or myth-systems, sometimes regarded as an attempt to "remythologize" experience as a reaction to perceived dehumanizing forces. Among fantasy narratives, J. R. R. Tolkien's *The Silmarillion* (1977) is a good example. The term has also been used by anthropologists and cultural historians to describe a world view and way of using language characteristic of preliterate, ritualistic, or "pre-logical" societies.

MYTHOS. Originally and literally, narrative or plot. Two radically different but specific meanings have been applied to this term in discussions of fantasy, neither of them, ironically, particularly related to this original Greek meaning: (1) In the sense employed by Northrop Frye, any aspect of the narrative of a work, and in particular one of four archetypal narrative patterns—comic, romantic, tragic, or ironic [92]. (2) In the usage popularized by H. P. Lovecraft, a body of stories based on some fundamental set of fantastic premises, as his own "Cthulhu mythos." Though the latter term potentially has broad applications in fantasy study, it is usually found only in discussions of Lovecraft's own body of work and pastiches by later writers.

N

NARRATIO FABULOSA. Perhaps the earliest critical attempt to define a genre of narrative similar to what is now called Speculative Fiction.* The fourth-century neoplatonic philosopher Macrobius, in his commentary on Cicero's *Dream of Scipio*, identified narratives that he called *narratio fabulosa*, which dealt with issues of natural philosophy in an exploratory way, rather than with the purely fictitious material and entertaining motives of Fables* [181].

NATURAL PRESENT. A term borrowed from E. R. Eddison by Waggoner and used to describe works whose settings differ from reality only in that magical forces or beings "actively operate on the lives of people" [199].

NEBULA AWARD. Annual awards for novels and short fiction presented since 1966 by the Science Fiction Writers of America,* whose membership votes on the awards.

NEGATIVE RELATIONALITY. The notion that fantasy achieves its effects by contravening or negating accepted notions of reality. Considered in terms of traditional realism, according to Rosemary Jackson, fantasy depends largely upon the impossible, the unreal, the invisible, etc. Jackson argues that this "negative relationality" "constitutes the meaning of the modern fantastic" [106]. See also ESTRANGEMENT; IMPOSSIBLE; NEGATIVE SUBJUNCTIVITY.

NEGATIVE SUBJUNCTIVITY. Used by Joanna Russ to describe the contravention of reality in fantasy: "Fantasy is what *could not have happened*" [165]. The idea is borrowed from Samuel R. Delany. See also SUBJUNCTIVITY.

NEOGOTHIC. The adaptation by later writers of elements originally associated with the Gothic Novel.* Leslie Fiedler referred to science fiction as a "neogothic" form [86], and a number of other critics have since noted the persistence of such elements in the genre. The term has on occasion been applied to modern Horror* fiction as well, particularly that which introduces traditionally Gothic elements into urban or contemporary settings.

NEOLUDDISM. See LUDDISM.

NEOPRIMITIVISM. An attitude, associated most often with the work of Edgar Rice Burroughs but sometimes applied to a broader range of fantastic literature from William Morris to Sword and Sorcery,* that rejects modern civilization as effete and emasculating and celebrates wilderness and warrior-hunter societies.

NEUROMANTIC. See CYBERPUNK.

NEW GEOGRAPHIES. Fantasies that take place in imaginary, but not necessarily supernatural, worlds [199]. See also HEROIC FANTASY.

NEW HISTORIES. Diana Waggoner's way of classifying works based on "alternate versions of primary history" [199]. See also ALTERNATE HISTORY.

NEW MAP. A frequently used metaphor for science fiction's techniques of Extrapolation* and Estrangement.* Although this phrase is now commonly associated with Kingsley Amis' 1960 study of science fiction *New Maps of Hell* (whose title Amis adapted from his own earlier poem, "Science Fiction") [8], the map metaphor as a means of describing science fiction's unique function in relation to Mainstream* literature was suggested as early as 1953, when Reginald Bretnor argued of "the impossibility of stretching the 'old maps' to fit the new terrain" [35]. The "new map" story later came to describe a very specific type of space travel narrative characterized, as Judith Merril described it, by a "detailed, sometimes highly technical, often very knowledgeable, explication of some as-yet unfilled-in area in a territory recently explored by the 'concept' and 'research' people, but open now to settlement and building-up by the 'engineering' and 'applications' men" [54].

NEW MYTHOLOGY. An oxymoron perhaps too often used to characterize science fiction's or fantasy's function or appeal. Variants are "contemporary mythology," "modern myth," or "twentieth-century mythology." Such terms possibly arise out of a desire to find cultural significance in a field that has seldom gained the serious attention of the dominant literary culture. The concept of science fiction as a modern analogue of myth probably became cemented in place with the publication in 1978 of *Science Fiction: Contemporary Mythology: The SFWA-SFRA Anthology* (Harper), edited by Patricia Warrick, Martin Harry Greenberg, and Joseph Olander. However, this anthology, like most criticism making mythic claims for science fiction, is characterized by some rather vague and unpersuasive claims: that science fiction covers some of the same concerns as earlier mythology, that science fiction stories are structured according to basic mythic patterns, or that favorite science fiction *themes* are—perhaps simply by virtue of their recurrence—to be regarded as myths. Earlier versions of this argument were presented by Philip Wylie, who described science fiction as a "modern mythology" in 1953 [35], and perhaps most importantly by Olaf Stapledon, who wrote in the preface to *Last and First Men* (1930), "We must achieve neither mere history, nor mere fiction, but myth" and described his novel as "an essay in myth creation." The most persuasive study examining this argument is Casey Fredericks' *The Future of Eternity: Mythologies of Science Fiction and Fantasy* [89].

NEWSSTAND FANTASY. Fantasy published in or associated with Pulp* magazines, as opposed to earlier traditions of Classical Fantasy,* according to Algis Budrys [41].

NEW WAVE. Françoise Giroud's term (*nouvelle vague*) to describe a group of younger French film directors who emerged in the late 1950s has since been enthusiastically appropriated by promoters of almost any unconventional movement within a popular art form previously characterized by conventions or formulae. In science fiction, the term was introduced by Judith Merril in a 1966 essay for *The Magazine of Fantasy and Science Fiction* ("Books," 30, no. 1 [January 1966]) to refer to the highly metaphorical and sometimes experimental fiction that began to appear in the English magazine *New Worlds* after Michael Moorcock assumed the editorship in 1964, and that was later popularized in the United States through Merril's own appallingly titled anthology *England Swings SF: Stories of Speculative Fiction* (Garden City: Doubleday, 1968). Although Harlan Ellison's anthology of original stories the preceding year (*Dangerous Visions*, Garden City: Doubleday, 1967) has sometimes been retroactively credited with unleashing the American version of the New Wave, and though Ellison spoke of the book as "a revolution" of "new horizons, new forms, new styles, new challenges," Ellison himself has expressed chagrin at having once been labeled the "chief prophet" of the New Wave in America (by *The New Yorker*: "The Talk of the Town: Evolution and Ideation" [September 16, 1967]). Similarly, many of the other writers associated with this movement, such as Brian Aldiss, J. G. Ballard, Thomas M. Disch, Samuel R. Delany, and Robert Silverberg, have on frequent occasions expressed disdain for or confusion over the term. Nevertheless, writers associated with the New Wave have been credited with introducing new narrative strategies into science fiction, with releasing the power of science fiction images as metaphor, and with weakening the boundaries that had long separated science fiction from Mainstream Fiction.*

NONCOGNITIVE ESTRANGEMENT. See COGNITIVE ESTRANGE-MENT.

NONMECHANISTIC. See MECHANISTIC.

NONSENSE. A variety of Whimsy,* usually in verse and characterized by meaningless words, logical paradoxes, and various impossibilities. Nonsense narratives are allied to fantasy in that they are usually fantastic, but the fantastic elements are generally the result of linguistic transformations rather than narrative conceptions.

NOVEL. The dominant modern genre of extended prose fiction. Most of the debates concerning whether the novel encompasses any long prose narrative or whether it properly concerns only the fictional representation of characters governed by the laws of probability (as opposed to Romance*) are so broadly drawn as to be of limited relevance to the history of generic science fiction and fantasy. To be sure, the works of such authors as William Morris or George MacDonald may have been excluded from the "novel" according to nineteenth-century standards of realism, and the early science fiction of H. G. Wells may have been termed Scientific Romances* for much the same reason, but by the twentieth century the novel had become as much a publisher's product as a theoretical genre, and for most modern writers the publishers' concerns have been highly relevant. In American popular science fiction, the novel-length narrative was practically unknown until after World War II; as a result, many Pulp* magazines would advertise "complete novels" that in fact might run no more than 15,000 words in length (although some later magazine editors might publish novels of 30–40,000 words). Even hardbound book publishers (Avalon being the most notable example) would publish novels of no more than 40,000 words. As a result, an informal definition of the science fiction novel emerged as anything long enough to be sold as a novel, whether in book or magazine form. This might include long magazine stories, Serials* published in book form, Fix-Ups* drawn from series of short stories, or even collections of stories with only slight connective tissue (such as Ray Bradbury's *The Martian Chronicles*). With the gradual liberation of science fiction and fantasy narratives from the vagaries of pulp editors and the dictates of trim sizes and page gatherings, however, *novel* came less to be defined according to word count or market strategies and more to be regarded as a narrative mode within the genres [43, 68].

NOVELET. A long story. Although sometimes defined as a short, light, and sentimental Short Novel*, and occasionally specified by Mainstream* magazines at lengths of approximately 15,000 words, "novelet" became a convenient term in science fiction and fantasy magazines for almost any story longer than the average but not long enough to be termed a Novel.* Traditionally, a novelet was defined as 10–20,000 words, although in some magazines "novelets" may have ranged from 5–12,000 words, anything longer being labeled a novel [43, 68].

NOVELIZATION. Originally, almost any novel-length narrative adapted from other narrative material (plays, biographies, myths, operas, etc.). The term now refers almost exclusively to novels written for a market generated by the film or television source materials from which the novels are adapted. Although the novelization is practically as old as the science fiction film—dating back at least to Thea von Harbou's novelized versions of her husband Fritz Lang's films *Metropolis* (1926; trans. 1927) and *A Girl in the Moon* (*Frau im Mond*, 1928, trans. *Rocket to the Moon*, 1929)—and although such well-known authors as Murray Leinster, Isaac Asimov, and Theodore Sturgeon have written in this form, it remains virtually unexplored critically. Novelizations are almost invariably dismissed as the most frankly commercial ventures in popular fiction (and indeed they can be among the most profitable), but at times they can provide interesting commentaries on their source material (such as William Kotzwinkle's 1982 novelization of the film *E.T.*) or represent a rethinking or recasting of the author's own earlier work (such as Peter George's 1963 novelization of the film *Dr. Strangelove*, which was itself based on his somewhat different earlier novel *Red Alert* [1958]).

NOVELLA. Originally a short story or tale, often specifically applied to early French or Italian writers such as Boccaccio. "Novella" eventually came also to be applied to works with greater character and theme development than the short story, but usually simpler plots than the Novel*—such as Joseph Conrad's "Heart of Darkness" (1902). The term entered the vocabulary of science fiction and fantasy editors and readers in the 1950s and may have been first used by Horace L. Gold of *Galaxy* magazine. Often, a "novella" in the science fiction magazines was indistinguishable from a Novelet,* but some editors would present novellas and novelets in the same issue, usually with the novella somewhat longer. By tradition, a novella ranged from 20,000 to 40-45,000 words.

NOVEL OF SCIENCE. A short-lived euphemism for science fiction. Donald A. Wollheim's *The Portable Novels of Science* (New York: Viking, 1945) was among the earliest hardbound anthologies of science fiction, and although Wollheim freely used the term "science fiction" in his introduction, "novels of science" appears to have been an early attempt at finding an alternative for this term in order to reach a more general audience.

NOVUM. A "strange newness" introduced into the experience of the reader of science fiction and generating the Estrangement* which Darko Suvin sees as defining the genre. Borrowing the term from Ernest Bloch, Suvin defines it further as "a totalizing phenomenon or relationship deviating from the author's and implied reader's norm of reality" [187].

NUMINA, NUMINOUS. Terms used primarily to refer to localized spirits or deities, to magical figures, or to the sense of the "wholly other" or "supramundane" as suggested by the German theologian Rudolph Otto, who coined this latter meaning in his 1917 study *Das Heilige* (trans. *The Idea of the Holy*). "Numinous" may thus describe the general sense of awe inspired by a fantasy narrative or various supernatural figures within the narrative. The term is sometimes confused with Kant's concept of *noumena*, or the "things-in-themselves" that lie beyond direct experience.

0

OCCULT FICTION. Fiction based in specific systems of mystical thought, or supernatural fiction in general. The notion of a secret reality that lies beyond the perceived world and is accessible through devices ranging from witchcraft to telepathy is a persistent one, and fiction based in such beliefs might seem to encompass a broad spectrum of fantasy and horror. In practice, however, "occult fiction" has been used to refer more narrowly to works by authors interested in particular occult beliefs, such as Edward Bulwer-Lytton or Marie Corelli; to (usually minor) works of fiction designed to dramatize the ideas of writers promoting particular systems of belief, such as those by Aleister Crowley or P. D. Ouspensky; or to fictions based in some popularly held belief or anxiety. The latter would include tales of witchcraft or demonic possession, for example, but not most Secondary World* fantasies or science fiction treatments of psychic or telepathic themes. As a contemporary marketing category, occult fiction includes such bestsellers as Ira Levin's *Rosemary's Baby* (1967) and William Peter Blatty's *The Exorcist* (1971).

OMNIPOTENCE OF THOUGHT. Freudian term referring to a fantasy that thinking about something may cause it to be so. Eric Rabkin has suggested that this fantasy is in some ways served by fantasy literature [157].

OPEN SYSTEM. See SYSTEMS MODEL.

ORGANIZED INNOCENCE. See FANTASY OF INNOCENCE.

ORIENTAL TALE. A style of fanciful narrative with Oriental settings in vogue during much of the eighteenth century. Early in that century, a number of translations and purported translations of tales from the

Arabic, Chinese, Turkish, and Persian appeared in England, and this soon gave rise to original tales with exotic Oriental settings. While many such tales (such as Samuel Johnson's *Rasselas*, 1754) were essentially philosophical-moral fictions, others tended more toward the sensational and became associated with the Gothic Novel.* The most notable example of this period was William Beckford's *Vathek* (1768), but the tradition of the Oriental tale survived in fantasy with works by later writers such as Ernest Bramah Smith.

OTHER. Widely used in philosophical and psychological writing to refer to the world outside of the self, or to hidden aspects of the self. The "other" or "not-I" has been identified by Rosemary Jackson as the fundamental semantic structure from which the various motifs of the fantastic are derived, with the "other" generally associated with themes of desire and the unconscious. "One of the central thrusts of the fantastic," she argues, is the attempt to erase the distinction between self and other [106].

OTHERWORLD. Term used by Ann Swinfen (and some other critics) to refer to what J. R. R. Tolkien calls the Secondary World.* Swinfen's usage somewhat more broadly includes the "otherworlds" of religious belief and received myth, however [189].

OTHER WORLD SCIENCE FICTION. Identified by Frank Cioffi as one of the three major Formulas* of stories that appeared in *Astounding* during the 1930s (the others being Status Quo* and Subversive* science fiction). "Other world science fiction" included stories that took place entirely in an imagined environment and therefore, according to Cioffi, represented a more sophisticated formula than the other types of stories, which were set against backgrounds of a recognizable social fabric [52].

OXFORD CHRISTIANS. Charles Moorman's description of the group of English writers associated with the Inklings* [137].

OXYMORON. The traditional rhetorical device of bringing together two contradictory terms in a single phrase, described by Rosemary Jackson as "the basic trope of fantasy" [106].

P

PAN-DETERMINISM. The notion that any element in a narrative may be causally related to any other element. Tzvetan Todorov argued that a characteristic of fantastic literature is the tendency to erase traditional distinctions between physical and mental, matter and spirit, word and object, resulting in a fictional universe in which causal relations might exist among all things and at all levels. Hidden laws might reveal unforeseen effects from any given cause; in a sense, anything might be influenced by or influence anything else [193]. Similar ideas have been expressed by other theorists. See also CONDITIONAL JOY; MIMESIS.

PANSIGNIFICATION. A logical corollary of Pan-Determinism,* according to Thomas H. Keeling: In a world in which anything might be causal, everything is charged with meaning and of indeterminate significance [181].

PARABLE. A story, usually short, that teaches a moral or religious lesson [93]. Often such tales include fantastic elements, and often the term is rather loosely employed to describe works of science fiction or fantasy that are Satires* or Cautionary Tales.*

PARADIGM. Used in two distinct senses in discussions of fantasy and—more often—science fiction; both usages are borrowed from fields other than literary criticism. First, the attitudes toward science and scientific progress expressed in works of science fiction may be discussed in terms of the dominant "paradigms" or world views as described by Thomas S. Kuhn in his 1962 study of the history of science, *The Structure of Scientific Revolutions*. According to Kuhn, science has not progressed linearly, but rather through a series of "revolutions" in which a dominant paradigm or set of assumptions would gradually give way to a newer paradigm; this use of the term has been adopted by Eric S. Rabkin [156], Gary K. Wolfe [208], and others in discussions of science fiction's relation to the science of its time.

In structual linguistics, a paradigm refers to the complex of words that exist as potential substitutes, or in a synchronic relationship to, individual words in a sentence. (Within the sentence, the words bear a "syntagmatic" or diachronic relationship to each other.) Semiotic theory has further defined these paradigms as "semantic fields" which may be further arrayed into given structures, such as binary oppositions. Given the unusual use of language in fantastic literature, with its often nonexistent referents or frames of reference, attempts at paradigmatic analysis have been undertaken by a number of critics. Mark Rose defined the principal paradigm of science fiction as the opposition of human and nonhuman interacting with a secondary opposition between science and nature [160]. Wolfe attempted a similar paradigm with his opposition of known and unknown [208]. Marc Angenot argued that since the fictive worlds and words of science fiction lacked paradigmatic relationships, a problem in discussions of the genre inevitably arises as readers are forced to resort to a "conjectural mode of reading" in which the absent paradigm is replaced by paradigms of the empirical world [9].

PARALITERATURE. (more common as the French *paralittérature*, and related to the German *Trivialliteratur*). Those genres of popular writing excluded from the accepted or "canonical" literature of the dominant class within a society. *Genre literature* and *popular literature* are more common terms in American popular culture scholarship. A bibliography of "paraliteratures" is Yvon Allard's *Paraliteratures* (Montreal, 1979), and a bibliography by Marc Angenot of studies of paraliterature appears in *Science-Fiction Studies* 13 (November 1977): 305–308). See also POPULAR CULTURE.

PARALLEL WORLDS. Sometimes applied to Alternate History,* sometimes to fantasy worlds conceived as invisibly coexisting with our own, and sometimes to the potentially infinite series of possible worlds implied by the so-called many worlds interpretation of quantum mechanics; hence, a theme shared equally by fantasy and science fiction.

PARAXIS. In optics, the region on either side of the central axis of a lens; in physiology, areas near the central axis of the body. Rosemary Jackson suggested that the fantastic bears a similar relationship to the "real," and that the "space" of the fantastic might be described as a "paraxis" which "is neither entirely 'real' (object), nor entirely 'unreal'

(image), but is located somewhere indeterminately between the two"
[106].

PASTORAL. From the Latin *pastor* (shepherd), and traditionally used
to describe a highly conventionalized kind of poetry, drama, and romance
in which human relationships are explored in idealized natural settings
[93]. Kathryn Hume has distinguished between "insider-pastoral," which
is presented from the point of view of an inhabitant of the idealized
landscape, and "outsider-pastoral," in which a hero tests himself in this
landscape before returning to his own world. Hume argues that "fantasy
pastoral is relatively rare," and cites as examples A. A. Milne's *Winnie
the Pooh* (1926) and Kenneth Grahame's *The Wind in the Willows* (1908)
[102]. Other critics, however, have argued that the pastoral impulse is
central to much modern fantasy, citing as evidence the often-idealized
rural settings and formal style.

PENNY DREADFUL. Perhaps the first genuine "mass market"
proletarian fiction in England. Penny dreadfuls (or "bloods" as they
were sometimes suggestively called) flourished from the 1840s to the
1860s. Morbid and sensational thrillers which were sold in serial form
at one to three pence per installment, the form led not only to endlessly
convoluted and repetitive plots on the part of its authors, but also to a
popularization and vulgarization of a number of Gothic* and fantastic
narrative traditions, which in turn may have contributed to the
development of modern sensational Horror* stories and films. Perhaps
the most famous penny dreadful, and one of the few to ever be reprinted,
is *Varney the Vampire* (1847), by either James Malcolm Rymer or Thomas
Peckett Prest.

PERCEPTUAL DISCONTINUITY. See ESTRANGEMENT.

PHANTASY. Rarely used anymore as an archaic spelling of "fantasy,"
but given a specific psychological meaning by C. G. Jung in his
Psychological Types (1921). "Each day a new reality is created by the
psyche," wrote Jung, and his term for this activity was "phantasy."
Phantasy may be active or passive, with passive phantasy characterized
by dreams and active phantasy characterized by artistic creation.

PHYSICS-FICTION. A term presumably referring to science fiction
which was used by Vladimir Nabokov in his 1969 novel *Ada*. Some
critics have since borrowed the term. In the same novel, Nabokov referred
to "technology fiction."

PLANET-BUILDING. Technique by which certain writers of Hard Science Fiction*—perhaps most notably Hal Clement—employ principles of astronomy, geology, meteorology, biology, and other sciences in calculating the likely conditions of an imaginary world in a science fiction narrative. The technique is similar to modeling in the geophysical sciences, but is perhaps more parallel to research conducted by historical novelists in that many of the details of the imaginary world may never appear in the final narrative. An interesting multi-author experiment in planet-building is *Medea: Harlan's World*, edited by Harlan Ellison (1985).

PLANET ROMANCE. A species of Proto Science Fiction* which achieved popularity initially in the seventeenth century and consisted of works that described societies on other planets, usually to some satiric or didactic purpose. Cyrano de Bergerac, Johannes Kepler, and Francis Godwin are among authors who wrote such narratives, which frequently were set on the moon. Such works probably influenced later satirists such as Swift, and the recurring popularity of the genre led to other precursors of science fiction such as C. I. Defontenay's 1854 novel *Star* [187].

PLAY. "Nonearnest" but structured activities that lie outside moral and cultural conventions, according to Johan Huizinga, whose theory of play has been cited by W. R. Irwin and others as a part of the reason for the appeal and cultural significance of fantasy [105].

POLITICAL SCIENCE FICTION. Broadly, any science fiction on political themes, as employed in the 1974 anthology *Political Science Fiction: An Introductory Reader*, edited by Martin H. Greenberg and Patricia Warrick. More narrowly, the term was employed by some reviewers in the 1960s to refer to an emerging Subgenre* of Bestsellers,* often only marginally science fiction through their near-future settings, which often dealt with political intrigue in Washington; the most prominent example of the period is probably Fletcher Knebel (*Seven Days in May* with Charles Bailey, 1962; *Night of Camp David*, 1965).

POLYSEMY. Multiplicity of meanings generated by a single text, characteristic of much symbolic fantasy that may support variant interpretations.

POPULAR CULTURE. Those aspects of cultural expression most influenced by commerce, formulaic structures, and broad appeal—or the interdisciplinary study of such aspects of culture. While science fiction is nearly always subsumed under this rubric (fantasy seems more problematical), "popular culture" is no more clearly defined in most discussions than is science fiction itself. The term seems to have largely supplanted "mass culture," which gained popularity among sociologists in the 1950s and is now disdained by some scholars as implicitly elitist, its opposite being "high culture" or "serious art." This distinction was largely based on the artist's supposed intent—"serious art" created for its intrinsic value, "popular art" for the marketplace. More recent scholars have tended more toward historical and economic definitions of the term, referring to high culture as that associated with the privileged classes and popular culture as that associated with the masses. But even this definition presents problems, in that virtually all written literature prior to the nineteenth century becomes high culture simply by virtue of limited literacy, and such achievements as Gothic cathedrals, often claimed as high culture, cannot realistically be said to have appealed to such a limited audience. Still more recently, many scholars have tended to agree with Russel Nye (*The Unembarrassed Muse*, 1970), who argued that popular culture in its modern sense is the product of the rise of an economically powerful middle class and the increase in literacy during the last 200 years. These developments made it possible for artists to survive economically by the sale of their works to a broad-based public rather than by patronage of a small but wealthy audience. Popular culture is also for this reason associated with technological developments ranging from high-speed presses to television.

While fantasy in the broadest sense can be said to have a place in narrative traditions of both "high" and "low" culture, modern generic fantasy and science fiction are clearly a product of this latter development—first through Penny Dreadfuls* or Dime Novels,* later through Pulp* magazines and film and television. A number of authors and critics of the genre have complained about the association of science fiction and fantasy with popular culture, and have often claimed a peculiar kind of elitism for the genres based on the nature of their readership. Such arguments sometimes confuse high culture with the Mainstream,* which is itself arguably as much a concept of popular culture as are popular genres. Recent scholarship, especially in science fiction study, has begun more openly to acknowledge the popular culture origins of the genre, and especially the degree to which for most of its history its development was economically driven by magazine and book sales, and at least indirectly by such unarguably popular culture phenomena as science fiction films and television series. See also FORMULA; GENRE; PARALITERATURE.

POSITIVISM. Introduced by the nineteenth-century French philosopher Auguste Comte to describe the belief that philosophical systems should be based on empirically verifiable and observable phenomena as described by scientific investigation. Opposed in general to metaphysical and religious thought, positivism attained its greatest influence during the nineteenth century in Europe, although it continued to have considerable impact in the United States until well into the twentieth century, and it has been identified by some critics (notably W. Warren Wagar) as the characteristic world view of such early science fiction writers as Jules Verne and H. G. Wells, and as the dominant view even today of advocates of Hard Science Fiction* [198]. Certainly, much of the editorializing of figures from John W. Campbell, Jr., to Isaac Asimov tends to support this view of a positivistic bias in much science fiction.

POSTHISTORY. Gene Wolfe's term for far future settings (such as in his own *Book of the New Sun*, 1980–1983) in which artifacts from the present or near future constitute a kind of fragmentary or semi-legendary history for the characters in that setting [211]. The term is obviously modeled on "prehistory" in that it refers to a culture in which what we view as continuous historical process and documentation has been fragmented or obliterated; the technique is fairly common in works that have been characterized as Medieval Futurism.*

POST-HOLOCAUST. Commonly applied to a variety of works set in the aftermath of a major cataclysm, usually a nuclear war, and often identified as a major Subgenre* of science fiction works that gained prominence after 1945 and have remained a staple of the field. See COSMIC DISASTER STORY; ESCHATOLOGICAL ROMANCE.

POST-MODERN. In Mainstream* literary history, the period roughly since 1965 [93], although the term was used as early as the 1930s in reference to Latin American literature, and although historian Arnold Toynbee identified the "postmodern" period of world history as beginning in 1875. What is widely called post-modern fiction is characterized by (among other things) a notable resurgence of the fantastic following the dominance of realism in the immediate postwar years. Authors associated with this period who have used devices of fantasy or science fiction include Thomas Pynchon, Kurt Vonnegut, Doris Lessing, John Fowles, Italo Calvino, Vladimir Nabokov, and Jorge Luis Borges.

POST-MODERN SCIENCE FICTION. Suggested by Algis Budrys as a characterization of 1950s science fiction, especially that published in *Galaxy* magazine and written by authors who had contributed to the growth of Modern Science Fiction* through contributions to *Astounding Science Fiction* during the period 1938–1950. In Budrys' own words, "the edges of this category are quite fuzzy and subjective" [43].

POST-SCIENTIFIC. A world view that questions or undermines the fundamental scientific notions of causality or observability, cited by Patrick Parrinder as characteristic of the work of Philip K. Dick and others [149]. See also IRRATIONALISM.

POST-STRUCTURALISM. A critical methodology based largely on the French critic Jacques Derrida's concept of "deconstruction," or the analysis of component parts of a given text in terms of various possible contexts, with emphasis shifted from author and text to reader, since the very uncertainty of language and its inability to represent reality calls the former into question. Examples of such methodologies in the study of fantastic literature may be found in the works of Samuel R. Delany [69] and Christine Brooke-Rose [38].

PREDICTION. In regard to fiction, an inference of possible future events as opposed to visionary Prophecy.* One might argue that prediction in this sense is more the function of science than of science fiction, given the principle of the replicability of experiments and the criterion that an adequate theory must predict certain observations. However, the term has been associated with science fiction so persistently in the popular media that it is unlikely to be banished, despite the vocal protests of most modern science fiction writers and critics. Although seldom proposed as a serious critical term or principle, prediction was nevertheless often cited as one of the functions of science fiction by such early advocates as Hugo Gernsback, and even recent popular accounts of the genre have found it difficult to resist recounting such nuggets as, say, the use of the term "atomic bomb" by H. G. Wells in 1914. See also EXTRAP-OLATION.

PREFIGURATION. Technique by which a text or idea system, such as a myth, provides an informed reader with a particular set of expectations which the author can then manipulate. The term, according to Casey Fredericks, derives from Biblical scholarship that depicted the Old Testament as a "prefiguration" of the New Testament [89]. Presumably, prefiguration could refer both to generally familiar materials, such as the Arthurian legends that provide a pattern of expectation in readers of Arthurian fantasy, and to particular generic conventions, such as those of Sword and Sorcery,* that prefigure the reader's experience of new works in a particular Subgenre.*

PREHISTORIC FICTION. Narratives concerning prehistoric characters and set in periods earlier than recorded history, according to Marc Angenot and Nadia Khouri [10]. Examples include Jack London's *Before Adam* (1906) and William Golding's *The Inheritors* (1955).

PREQUEL. A work describing earlier events involving characters or settings from a previous work. C. S. Lewis' *The Magician's Nephew* (1955) is a prequel to his earlier "Narnia" books in that it describes the origins of Narnia.

PRIMARY BELIEF. Belief in the world as experienced, as opposed to Secondary Belief* as described by J. R. R. Tolkien [194].

PRIMITIVISM. Usually, the romanticization of earlier phases of social or even biological development. Almost always used in a thematic rather than a stylistic sense, primitivism in science fiction and fantasy includes those stories that focus on reverse evolution (such as Robert Louis Stevenson's "Dr. Jekyll and Mr. Hyde," 1886), on the re-emergence of pre-Christian or even pre-human powers (as in works by Arthur Machen or H. P. Lovecraft), on Lost Races,* or on future societies reverting to medievalism or barbarism (including what John Carnell has termed Medieval Futurism*). These and a variety of other themes are discussed by Casey Fredericks under the general topic of "return to the primitive," which suggests the appeal of the simpler ways of life represented by such imaginary events or societies [89]. The deliberate rejection of modern social and economic structures in favor of more elementally heroic environments, as in the work of Edgar Rice Burroughs, has been termed "neoprimitivism" by Thomas D. Clareson [53], and W. Warren Wagar has discussed primitivism in the context of eschatology under the rubric Edenism* [198].

PROLEPSIS. In rhetoric, the device by which an opponent's argument may be anticipated and countered in advance, thus reducing the argument's effectiveness. (The term may also mean a preliminary statement to a more detailed argument.) By extension, the term has been applied to narratives that anticipate future events or treat future events as past; thus much science fiction has been on occasion described as "proleptic," and prolepsis identified as a major rhetorical device of the genre. Finally, the term is sometimes invoked to mean the narrative device of the "flash-forward," as opposed to the "flashback" (or *analepsis*).

PROPHECY. In literary usage, works suggestive of divine inspiration. Although prophetic or visionary literature is sometimes included in a broad definition of fantasy, and although certain fantasy works may be properly described as comparable to the "prophetic" works of poetic tradition, E. M. Forster makes a distinction between the two based primarily on tone. The prophetic tone, he argues, implies religious belief or the presence of supernatural forces, while fantasy makes manifest such forces, often at the expense of unity of vision. Forster's examples of the latter include Dostoevsky and Melville [87]. (See also Fantastic-Prophetical Axis.*) In science fiction history, "prophecy" was given a particular meaning by H. G. Wells, who used it to refer to the device of pointing up problems of contemporary society by projecting them into the future as fantasy, such as in his own *The Time Machine* (1895). Wells' use of the term is akin to the more widespread Extrapolation* [150].

PROTOCOL. A learned code or procedure for reading certain kinds of texts. The notion that science fiction or fantasy comprises ways of reading rather than bodies of texts has been discussed by a number of critics, but most significantly by Samuel R. Delany, who argues that a genre is "not a set of texts or of rhetorical figures but rather a reading protocol complex" [72]. Essentially, a protocol (originally from a Greek word referring to the first page of a scroll of papyrus in which the nature and authenticity of the scroll are verified) consists of those assumptions in reading that the reader brings to the text, and that are signaled early in the text itself (or possibly in the context in which the text appears). The protocols of science fiction reading, then, would result in a literal reading of a statement that might appear metaphorical or hallucinatory in a "realistic" or Mundane* text.

PROTO SCIENCE FICTION. Used in *The Science Fiction Encyclopedia* as a general term for referring to science fiction–like works that preceded the existence of a recognizable genre of science fiction [144], and therefore similar to Brian Aldiss' Ur-Science Fiction.* Brian Stableford [144] argues that proto science fiction effectively ends with the beginning of a continuous tradition in 1818, with the publication of Mary Shelley's *Frankenstein*, and Peter Nicholls, who apparently coined the term, has elsewhere argued that "proto science fiction" ends sometime in the early nineteenth century with the Industrial Revolution [143].

PSEUDOMYTH. Artificial myths, cast as fantasy narratives and including such works as Olaf Stapledon's *The Flames* (1947) and Walter M. Miller, Jr.'s *A Canticle for Leibowitz* (1959), according to Darko Suvin [187].

PSEUDONATURAL. R. D. Mullen's term for fantastic beings lacking supernatural powers—talking animals, centaurs, griffins, brownies, trolls, superhumans such as Tarzan or Conan, "in sum, all unnatural things with merely natural powers however much exaggerated" [141].

PSEUDOSCIENCE. Generally used to refer to theories or systems that employ scientific terminology and sometimes gain wide popular acceptance even when dismissed as unverifiable or unsubstantiated by the scientific community at large. Until about 1950, the term was often used by librarians as an alternative to science fiction [118], much to the chagrin of many writers, but in fact a number of science fiction narratives have been based on pseudoscientific notions, such as the series of "psionic" stories encouraged by John W. Campbell, Jr., in *Astounding* in the early 1950s.

PSI. Possibly derived from "psionics," a coinage associated with John W. Campbell, Jr., in the early 1950s and referring to hidden powers of the human mind (originally, as revealed through technological devices). "Psi" has gained wide usage in Fandom* and in some criticism as shorthand for the whole complex of science fiction stories dealing with telepathy, telekinesis, etc. Generally, its usage seems to be to signify such themes when treated in a science fiction context, as opposed to fantasy or supernatural literature.

PSYCHOHISTORY. In common use since the 1960s to refer to the use of psychotherapeutic or psychoanalytic methodologies in the study of individual biographies or mass movements such as witchcraft or millenialism. In science fiction, however, this term has retained a quite different meaning through its use by Isaac Asimov in his *Foundation* series (1942–1949). In this work, psychohistory was described as a statistical science (perhaps based on a crude form of Marxism) that attempted to formulate laws "to govern and predict the mass action of human groups." The term has not been widely adopted by other writers, although the concept is not unique to Asimov.

PSYCHOMACHIA. A narrative depicting a conflict of personified vices and virtues, as in the fourth-century Latin poet Prudentius' long poem of this title. Since then, the term has come to be widely used to refer to allegorical portrayals of battles between good and evil, and thus has been adopted by Ann Swinfen [189] and others in discussions of fantasy narratives.

PSYCHOMYTH. Term used by Ursula K. Le Guin to describe those of her stories that lack identifiable historical or science fictional referents, "more or less surrealistic tales, which share with fantasy the quality of taking place outside any history, outside of time, in that region of the living mind which—without invoking any consideration of immortality—seems to be without spatial or temporal limits at all" [114].

PULP. Originally a kind of cheap, acidic wood-pulp paper, but now more often used to refer to the magazines published on such paper, which attained a collective circulation of nearly 10 million per issue during the 1930s, according to Russel Nye (*The Unembarrassed Muse*, 1970). More broadly, the term came to characterize the fiction and illustrations published in those magazines, and finally any fiction or illustrations making use of the conventions of pulp forms. The invention of the pulp magazine is generally credited to Frank Munsey, who in 1896 decided to convert his children's magazine *Golden Argosy* to a popular all-fiction magazine titled *Argosy*, and switched to cheap untrimmed wood-pulp paper in order to keep the price low. Pulp magazines are of particular importance to the history of American fantasy in that, beginning with *Weird Tales* in 1923, they provided a focal point, consolidated an audience, and began to establish conventions and formulas for several Subgenres* of fantasy, especially Horror* fiction and Sword and Sorcery.* Science fiction pulps were equally successful, and many historians of the genre have dated its beginning as a self-conscious genre from the founding of *Amazing Stories* by Hugo Gernsback in 1926. Western, romance, detective, aviation, and war story pulps also flourished, but magazines devoted to other subgenres (such as *Oriental Tales*, begun in 1930) did not fare as well. John W. Campbell, Jr.'s *Unknown*, begun in 1939, did much to develop a modern popular genre of logical and often humorous fantasy parallel to science fiction, and such pulps as *Famous Fantastic Mysteries* and *The Avon Fantasy Reader* were instrumental in creating a younger audience for older Lost Race Fantasies* and horror fiction. By the mid–1950s, most pulp magazines had been replaced by Digest* size magazines, although critics and historians have since sometimes used the term to refer to any sensational formulaic fiction.

Q

QUEST. While some would argue that the quest is a defining feature of much fantasy literature, this term is sometimes used to distinguish those narratives in which a traditionally mounted quest is the central element of plot. See also ANTI-QUEST.

R

RADICAL DISCONTINUITY. The dislocation between the imagined world of romance or fantasy and the world of experience. Although Robert Scholes implies that such a discontinuity is "at the root of all narrative structure," it becomes more apparent in "pure romance" [176].

RATIONALIZED FANTASY. A term used by Roger Schlobin and others to describe narratives that employ fantasy conventions but rationalize the fantasy elements through devices of psychology or science fiction [170].

RATIONAL SUPERNATURAL. Works in which apparently supernatural events are in the end explained through illusions, tricks, hypnosis, etc. See also RATIONALIZED FANTASY.

REALISM OF PRESENTATION. "The art of bringing something close to us, making it palpable and vivid, by sharply observed or sharply imagined detail." C. S. Lewis uses this term in opposition to "realism of content" in nonfantastic fiction [120].

REALISTIC FANTASY. Julius Kagarlitski described as realistic fantasy those works that, emerging principally in the 1860s and 1870s and most prominently represented by Jules Verne, began with a single fantastic assumption which was then "verified" by numerous devices of exposition and action, and which provided the basis for otherwise "realistic" narrative developments. Eventually, this genre came to be known as science fiction [54].

RECOVERY. "Regaining of a clear view," according to J. R. R. Tolkien, who includes in this the return and renewal characteristic of the endings of fairy stories [194]. See also CONSOLATION; ESCAPE; FANTASY.

RED DETECTIVE. A Subgenre* of postrevolutionary Russian science fiction thrillers, usually concerning the export of the Soviet revolution to other parts of the world with the aid of new inventions or weapons [142].

RESISTANCE STORY. A group of science fiction stories that share the theme of an underground resistance movement working to liberate a conquered United States; although this very narrow definition was given by Martin H. Greenberg and Joseph D. Olander [204], the term also has a broader meaning in non–science fiction genres such as the war story, where it refers to any tale of organized resistance to an oppressive regime.

REVERIE. In Gaston Bachelard's sense (*The Poetics of Reverie*, 1960), distinct from a dream in that it involves a state of mind that situates us "in a world and not in a society." Bachelard's use of this term has occasionally been invoked in discussions of fantastic literature; see, for example, William F. Touponce's *Ray Bradbury and the Poetics of Reverie* [195].

REVERSAL. Classically, *peripety* or sudden change in fortune for a protagonist. In discussions of fantastic literature, reversal often denotes the techniques by which reader expectations or assumptions are controverted by apparent impossibilities, suggesting a "reversal" of the accepted Ground Rules* of reality or causality. See also ANTI-EXPECTED; IMPOSSIBLE.

REVISION. Most obviously, the process of altering or rewriting an earlier text. Kathryn Hume, however, has suggested that a "literature of revision" is opposed to a "literature of vision" in that the former provides a model for changes of existing reality, whereas the latter constructs an entirely new reality; science fiction, then, often partakes of the "literature of revision," whereas (very broadly) fantasy may partake more often of the literature of vision [102].

ROBINSONADE. An imitation or pastiche of *Robinson Crusoe* (1719). The enormous popularity of Daniel Defoe's tale of a desert island castaway gave rise to so many imitations that a scant twelve years after its publication the German critic Johann Gottfried Schnabel invented this term to describe the genre; occasionally, "prerobinsonade" has been used to describe such works published before Defoe's work [95]. A number of robinsonades introduced clearly fantastic elements and thus belong to the history of fantasy, but a number of critics have also pointed out the major themes of survival, isolation, ingenuity, and the "white man's burden" that *Robinson Crusoe* shares with much science fiction, and science fiction has indeed produced a number of robinsonades of its own, such as Rex Gordon's *First on Mars* (1956).

ROBOTICS. See LAWS OF ROBOTICS.

ROMANCE. Apart from its historical meanings and the various scholarly debates over the romance as distinguished from the novel, this term has popularly come to mean any fiction involving an idealized world or idealized characters (probably after Northrop Frye [92]) or a specific market genre involving romantic relationships in exotic settings. In the first sense, most of fantastic literature would be subsumed by the genre, as well as most popular genres such as the western, the detective story, the heroic fantasy, or science fiction. See FANTASTIC ROMANCE.

S

SACRAMENTALISM. The belief that all nature is full of spiritual meaning, symbolic of an unseen world. C. S. Lewis speculated that if the material world is "the copy of an invisible world," then "sacramentalism" or Symbolism* involves "the attempt to read that something else through its sensible imitations" [119]. Later critics such as Charles Moorman have adopted the term to refer to writers such as Lewis himself; according to Moorman, sacramentalism involves a mode of representation in which the vehicle and tenor of the metaphor are identified, with no essential difference between the symbol and that which is symbolized [137].

SACRED TIME. The primordial or magic time in which the events of myth take place. Although usually conceived of as apart from historical time, sacred time often implies an indeterminate past; thus the events of sacred time can provide a model for behavior in historical time, according to Mircea Eliade. Actors in sacred time are characteristically supernatural beings [79].

SAGA. Originally a family history or genealogical tale from oral tradition (and still occasionally used in almost that sense, as with John Galsworthy's *The Forsyte Saga*). The term is often associated with Icelandic narratives in which supernatural events and mythological figures are incorporated into the genealogical material. In discussions of fantasy, "saga" usually refers to narratives that in setting, atmosphere, or structure resemble materials from Norse traditions, such as Poul Anderson's *Hrolf Kraki's Saga* (1973). In science fiction, the term is used considerably more loosely to refer to almost any large-scale narrative with mythic implications, such as Julian May's *Saga of Pliocene Exile* (1981–1984).

SATIRE. A work that seeks to improve human behavior or human institutions through devices of wit, humor, or exaggeration. Satire has since classical times employed devices of fantasy, and some writers have even traced the beginnings of science fiction to this tradition, particularly to the second-century *A True History* of Lucian of Samosata. Peter Nicholls has argued that the most common function of the imaginary environments of Proto Science Fiction* was satirical [144], and a satirical edge remained in many of the Scientific Romances* of H. G. Wells— for example, the implicit (and sometimes explicit) criticism of English class structure in *The Time Machine*. Most dystopian and Anti-Utopian* fiction is essentially satirical, and perhaps because of the predominance of these works fantastic satire has come to be more closely associated with the classic "Juvenalian" mode of biting ridicule of human follies (as opposed to the gentler "Horatian" satire, which occasionally characterizes Satiric Fantasy* such as that which appeared in John W. Campbell, Jr.'s *Unknown*).

Although science fiction satire for much of the Golden Age* was relatively mild, occasionally featured in the works of such writers as Henry Kuttner, it came to fruition with the founding of *Galaxy* magazine under the editorship of H. L. Gold in 1950. Among the most famous satires to first appear in that magazine were the stories that later became Ray Bradbury's *Fahrenheit 451* (1953) and Frederik Pohl and C. M. Kornbluth's *The Space Merchants* (1952). The 1950s saw many such works, but with increasingly complex narrative modes introduced into the genre in the 1960s and 1970s, satire came more and more to be incorporated into the larger arsenal of literary devices available to authors in the genre, and while many of the New Wave* authors employed satire, it was often in the context of broader and sometimes experimental narrative techniques. Some critics maintain that satire remains the most important characteristic of science fiction (see Comic Inferno*), or that all science fiction involving imaginary or future societies is at least implicitly satirical—in fact, a similar argument might be made for much fantastic literature in general, with its powerful elements of Desire* and Estrangement.*

SATIRIC FANTASY. Broadly, any work of fantasy with a satirical intent, such as the stories of John Collier or novels such as Fletcher Pratt and L. Sprague de Camp's 1940 *The Incomplete Enchanter* (with its various descendants down to the present popularity of such writers as Robert Asprin) or Charles G. Finney's *The Circus of Dr. Lao* (1935). Satiric fantasy has perhaps been less common in popular genre fiction than these works might suggest, but it was a fairly regular feature of John W. Campbell, Jr.'s magazine *Unknown* (1939–1943). T. E. Apter has used the term in a more specialized sense to denote works in which the fantastic element becomes a device in a larger satirical context, as in Nikolai Gogol's "The Nose" [11].

SCIENCE ADVENTURE. According to Algis Budrys, a term probably coined by Malcom Reiss of Love Romances Publishing Company to describe *Planet Stories* magazine (1939–1955) [43]. Although the term survived for some years as a publishing subcategory in the Pulps,* the more generally accepted term for this type of fiction is Space Opera,* even though the latter term was actually coined to refer to fiction of the 1930s.

SCIENCE DOMINANT. See ADVENTURE DOMINANT.

SCIENCE FANTASY. A rather imprecise term sometimes used interchangeably with science fiction, sometimes to refer to Sword and Sorcery,* sometimes to Sword and Planet,* and sometimes to Rationalized Fantasy.* Anthologist Judith Merril, who may have done more than anyone else to popularize the term through her consistent use of it in a long series of anthologies in the 1950s, seemed to prefer it as a generic term that blurred the boundaries between science fiction and fantasy, and thus permitted the inclusion of both kinds of stories in these anthologies (one of which, *SF: The Year's Greatest Science Fiction and Fantasy*, 1956, even used the clumsy term "science-fantasy-fiction"). In recent years, this usage has been generally supplanted by SF,* a term also pioneered by Merril.

More generally, when "science fantasy" is used to refer to science fiction, the term implies a generic categorization of science fiction as a branch of fantasy; when used to denote a somewhat separate body of works, it refers to a genre in which devices of fantasy are employed in a "science-fictional" context (related to but distanced from the "real world" by time, space, or dimension). Darko Suvin calls science fantasy a "misshapen subgenre" including Edgar Allan Poe, Abraham Merritt, and Ray Bradbury, and cites James Blish's criticism that the Subgenre* is really a variety of science fiction in which plausibility is only maintained until the author chooses or needs to discard it for purposes of plot [187]. Algis Budrys characterizes the genre by its introduction of fantasy elements into science fiction milieus (or "milieus where such science fiction signatures as rocketships and ray guns also occur") and claims it is usually a blend of fantasy and "science adventure," or Space Opera* [43]. A general discussion of science fantasy as a separate genre is Brian Attebery's essay "Science Fantasy" [18].

SCIENCE FICTION. Often regarded as a subset of fantasy, science fiction has been defined so frequently that there is little critical consensus as to which works might be included or excluded. Most definitions include the elements of scientific content (which may include concepts associated with scientific theory even when little or no science is present in the narrative), social extrapolation, and some cognitive or nonmetaphorical link to the "real world." The Ground Rules* of science fiction are essentially those of the physical universe, although they may include rules as yet undiscovered, whereas the ground rules of fantasy are generally said to be limited only by internal consistency and not necessarily related to experience.

Like fantasy (but more so), science fiction gained its identity as a commercial term for category fiction in magazines and books long before literary scholarship and genre theory began attempting to define it; as a result, most definitions have proved unsatisfactory to some readers, and one of the most popular definitions remains Damon Knight's "what we point to when we say it" (1952) [110]. Although the term "science fiction" has been found as early as 1851 (in an essay by the minor English poet William Wilson, referring to "fiction in which the revealed truths of Science may be given interwoven with a pleasing story"), and although similar terms in other languages have been cited as early usages (such as the Swedish *naturvetenskaplig roman*, which according to Sam Lundwall appeared in 1916 [125]), popular usage probably dates from no earlier than 1929. In an editorial for the first issue of *Science Wonder Stories* in that year, Hugo Gernsback used the term to replace his earlier, rather awkward portmanteau Scientifiction,* which he had used in 1926 to describe the contents of his first magazine, *Amazing Stories.* (Gernsback lost control of the latter magazine in bankruptcy proceedings early in 1929.)

Generally, the definitions offered over the years have fallen into three general categories: (1) early editor and fan definitions, which often stress the scientific, prophetic, and didactic elements of the genre, and which some later writers have come to refer to as "Gernsback's folly"; (2) definitions from practicing writers, which range from grandiose claims of the genre as virtually the only worthwhile modern literature to more practical definitions emphasizing publishing and marketing considerations; and (3) academic definitions, which frequently focus on rhetoric, reader response, and relationships to other genres. Until the past few years, most definitions in each category contained a substantial element of public relations as well as critical thought; owing to the commercial origins of the genre and the perceived low esteem in which it was held, those undertaking to define it often disguised within their definitions *apologia* for the genre, with the result that some definitions seemed to excessively stress the "human" element (as an implied counter to frequent perceptions of the genre as mechanistic), while others (such as Aldiss' and del Rey's below) even omitted concerns of fiction or narrative altogether, presenting science fiction instead as a kind of philosophical attitude or way of thinking. Some examples of these definitions:

Hugo Gernsback (defining scientifiction in 1926): "A charming romance intermingled with scientific fact and prophetic vision" [178].

J. O. Bailey (1947): "A narrative of an imaginary invention or discovery in the natural sciences and consequent adventures and experiences" [19].

Theodore Sturgeon (1951): "A story built around human beings, with a human problem and a human solution, which would not have happened at all without its scientific content." (Sturgeon later commented that this widely quoted "definition" was in fact intended to be a description of a *good* science fiction story [97].)

Kendall Foster Crossen (1951): "An imaginative exploration of any fact or theory within the realm of knowledge" ("Houyhnmhnms & Company," introduction to his anthology *Adventures in Tomorrow* [New York: Greenberg, 1951]).

Isaac Asimov (1952): "That branch of literature which is concerned with the impact of scientific advance upon human beings" [35]. (In 1975, Asimov essentially repeated this definition, altering it slightly to refer to literature that "deals with the reaction of human beings to changes in science and technology." A further revision in 1978 specified literature that "deals with human responses to changes in the level of science and technology" [14].

John W. Campbell, Jr. (1953): "The literature of speculation as to what changes may come, and which changes will be improvements, which destructive, which merely pointless" [35].

Rosalie Moore (1953): "Any fiction based on an exploration of or application of any existing or *imaginable* science, or extrapolation from the same" [35].

Reginald Bretnor (1953): Works that "reveal the author's awareness of the importance of the scientific method as a human function and of the human potentialities inherent in its exercise, and do this not only in plot and circumstance, but also *through the thoughts and motivations of the characters*"; or works that reveal such awareness "only in circumstance and plot" or only through presenting "certain potential *products* of the scientific method" [35]. (While Bretnor originally intended this to describe three broad classes of narrative encompassed by science fiction, Robert Heinlein in 1957 endorsed this definition while erroneously paraphrasing it to mean an "indispensable three-fold awareness" as a criterion of science fiction [67]; ironically, Heinlein's paraphrase has been more often reprinted than Bretnor's original definition.)

Basil Davenport (1955): "Fiction based upon some imagined development of science, or upon the extrapolation of a tendency in society" [66].

Robert Heinlein (1957): "Realistic speculation about possible future events, based solidly on adequate knowledge of the real world, past and present, and on a thorough understanding of the nature and significance of the scientific method" [67].

Kingsley Amis (1960): "That class of prose narrative treating of a situation that could not arise in the world we know, but which is hypothesized on the basis of some innovation in science or technology, or pseudo-science or pseudo-technology, whether human or extraterrestrial in origin" [8].

Sam Moskowitz (1963): "A branch of fantasy identifiable by the fact that it eases the 'willing suspension of disbelief' on the part of its readers by utilizing an atmosphere of scientific credibility for its imaginative speculations in physical science, space, time, social science, and philosophy" [138].

Robin Scott Wilson (1970): "A fiction in which science, or some credible extrapolation of science, is integrally combined with an honest consideration of the human condition" [205].

Robert M. Philmus (1970): A "rhetorical strategy" that "differs from other kinds of fantasy by virtue of the more or less scientific basis, real or imaginary, theoretical or technological, on which the writer predicates a fantastic state of affairs" [150].

Thomas D. Clareson (1971): "That type of fiction which results from and reflects, often topically, the impact of scientific theory and speculation upon the literary imagination—and, therefore, the effect of science upon people" [118].

Lester del Rey (1971): "An attempt to deal rationally with alternate possibilities in a manner which will be entertaining" [74].

Harlan Ellison (1971): "Anything that deals in even the smallest extrapolative manner with the future of man and his societies, with the future of science and/or its effects on us, with fantasy as an interpretation of the realities with which we are forced to deal daily" [118].

Donald A. Wollheim (1971): "That branch of fantasy which, while not true of present-day knowledge, is rendered plausible by the reader's recognition of the scientific possibilities of it being possible at some future date or at some uncertain period in the past" [212].

Brian W. Aldiss (1973): "The search for a definition of man and his status in the universe which will stand in our advanced but confused state of knowledge (science), and is characteristically cast in the Gothic or post-Gothic mould" [1].

Norman Spinrad (1973): "Science fiction is anything published as science fiction" ("Introduction" to his anthology *Modern Science Fiction* [Garden City: Anchor, 1974]).

Robert H. Canary (1974): "A fictive history laid outside what we accept as historical reality but operating by the same essential rules as that reality" [46].

Alan E. Nourse (1974): "Predominantly a speculative literature in which the reader is invited to ponder in some detail the effect that a given advance, change, discovery, or technological breakthrough might have upon society as we know it and upon human beings as we know them" [36].

Reginald Bretnor (again, in 1974): "Fiction based on rational speculation regarding the human experience of science and its resultant technologies" [36].

James Gunn (1975): Fiction in which "a fantastic event or development is considered rationally" [97].

Robert Scholes (defining structural Fabulation,* 1975): "A fictional exploration of human situations made perceptible by the implications of recent science" [174].

Eric S. Rabkin (1976): A work is science fiction "if its narrative world is at least somewhat different from our own, and if that difference is apparent against the background of an organized body of knowledge" [156].

Paul A. Carter (1977): "Science fiction is an imaginative extrapolation from the known into the unknown" [48].

Darko Suvin (1979): "A literary genre whose necessary and sufficient conditions are the presence and interaction of estrangement and cognition, and whose main formal device is an imaginative framework alternative to the author's empirical environment" [186].

Thomas H. Keeling (1979): "A form of fiction that, unlike confessional or psychological fiction, focuses on man's relationship with his natural and man-made environments and that, unlike such works as *The Faerie Queene*, assumes that the scientific perspective—even though it is imperfect and is the frequent cause of our crises—is still our best tool in dealing with those environments" [181].

Algis Budrys (1980): A "commercial genre" of stories "set in milieus where physical laws are held inviolate although the stories themselves may err, or deliberately elide such laws in order to function as stories." (Alternatively, Budrys offers the definition of "a body of general literature" which fans identify as science fiction.) [43]

W. Warren Wagar (1982, defining "speculative literature"): "Any work of fiction, including drama and narrative poetry, that specializes in plausible speculation about life under changed but rationally conceivable circumstances, in an alternative past or present, or in the future" [198].

David Hartwell (1984, defining "what science fiction means to insiders"): "The sum of all examples and all possible examples. Science fiction is every SF story written or to be written, the sum total of science fictional reality past, present, and future—otherwise indefinable" [99].

Northrop Frye, Sheridan Baker, and George Perkins (1985): "Fiction in which new and futuristic scientific developments propel the plot" [93].

Useful and insightful discussions of the problems with many of these definitions, and the problems inherent in attempting to define science fiction in general, may be found in Damon Knight's essay "What Is Science Fiction?" [111] and in Budrys' "Literatures of Milieux" [41]. See also SCIENCE FANTASY; SF; SPECULATIVE FICTION.

SCIENCE FICTION LEAGUE. A fan organization founded in 1934 by Hugo Gernsback and sponsored by *Wonder Stories* magazine. The organization is often credited with having provided a self-conscious identity for Fandom* and, to a more limited extent, for science fiction itself.

SCIENCE FICTION MYSTERY. Generally used to apply to a hybrid Subgenre* in which the plot elements of mystery or detective fiction are superimposed on a science fiction setting; the most famous example is probably Isaac Asimov's *The Naked Sun* (1957). However, the term has occasionally been invoked to refer to tales of "scientific" detectives, such as were published in Hugo Gernsback's magazine *Scientific Detective Monthly* (1930) or, more rarely, to the few mystery novels (the first of which was Anthony Boucher's *Rocket to the Morgue*, 1942) dealing with the world of science fiction writers and fans. A brief bibliography appears in Robert A. Baker and Michael T. Nietzel, "The Science Fiction Detective Story: Tomorrow's Private Eyes" [20].

SCIENCE FICTION RESEARCH ASSOCIATION. Academic organization founded in October 1970 with the goals of promoting scholarship, teaching, research, and archiving of science fiction, primarily through annual conferences held since 1971.

SCIENCE FICTION WESTERN. A story that consciously makes use of the conventions of both science fiction and western genres. Although science fiction is often identified as a kind of "frontier" literature, this term usually refers only to a deliberate cross-fertilization of these two popular genres. Examples include John Jakes' *Six-Gun Planet* (1970), H. Beam Piper's *A Planet for Texans* (1958), and John Boyd's *The Andromeda Gun* (1974). A study that discusses the relationship of science fiction to westerns is David Mogen's *Wilderness Visions* (1982); one more narrowly focused on science fiction westerns themselves is Robert Murray Davis, "The Frontiers of Genre: Science-Fiction Westerns," *Science-Fiction Studies* 35 (March 1985): 33–41.

SCIENCE FICTION WRITERS OF AMERICA. Organization of professional science fiction writers formed in 1965, largely as an outgrowth of the Milford Science Fiction Writers' Conference. The association sponsors the annual Nebula Awards,* although its focus is primarily on professional and legal issues affecting the writing profession. An earlier organization using the same initials (SFWA) was founded in 1952 in Los Angeles as the Science-Fantasy Writers of America.

SCIENTIFIC FANTASY. (translation of common Russian term for science fiction). See FANTASTIKA.

SCIENTIFIC METHOD. The traditional investigative logic of the natural sciences. Although Reginald Bretnor has made awareness of this method of inductively formulating and testing hypotheses a condition of his definition of science fiction [35], and although other writers have on occasion stressed the importance of the method in their advice to young writers, the fact is that relatively little fiction has focused on it in any important way, and the relationship of the scientific method to science fiction has not been a major critical concern within the genre. Nevertheless, it has on occasion provided a convenient structuring device for "puzzle" stories (and occasionally more sophisticated works) and has sometimes played a significant role in fiction that deals with the actual practice of working scientists. When the term is used, it is almost always in the traditional inductivist sense, with little awareness of the attacks on inductivism from philosophers such as Karl Popper.

SCIENTIFIC NOVEL. Term used by a writer in the New York *Herald* in 1835 to describe the "new species of literature" invented by Richard Adams Locke in his story published that year titled "The Moon Hoax"; cited by David Hartwell as an early definition of what came to be science fiction [99].

SCIENTIFIC ROMANCE. Used at least as early as 1886 for C. H. Hinton's series of speculative essays and short stories (*Scientific Romances*, 1888 and 1896), but now almost universally associated with the early science fiction novels of H. G. Wells. Wells himself used the term to distinguish these works from his later, Utopian* fictions. The term is perhaps less paradoxical today than it might have seemed in Wells' time, for the traditions of romance writing are more fully integrated with notions of progress than they were in the 1890s, when the English romance under such authors as Haggard and William Morris seemed decidedly anti-industrial and even antiscientific: A "scientific romance," then, appeared a kind of contradiction in terms. Although there have been few attempts to define this genre apart from general definitions of science fiction, Carlo Pagetti has suggested that the scientific romance is a "mixed literary genre combining the romantic tale of the journey into a lost land, Gothic sensationalism concerning mystery and death, and the expositional didacticism of philosophical speculation vulgarized for the benefit of the masses" [146]. The term is also used sometimes to refer specifically to science fiction published in the Munsey chain of magazines in the years surrounding World War I.

SCIENTIFICTION. Coined by Hugo Gernsback as a portmanteau of his earlier "scientific fiction" and used by him during the early years of *Amazing Stories*. The term was generally abandoned during the 1930s (Gernsback himself using the term "science fiction" for his 1929 *Wonder Stories*) and has come to suggest, as Algis Budrys notes, "science fiction with a primary emphasis on specific technological devices," often characterized by a primitive writing style and " 'travelogue' plot construction" [43]. Despite its awkwardness, "scientifiction" survived in letter columns and editorials of the Pulp* magazines for the next two decades, and was even the title of an early British Fanzine* in 1937. Occasional attempts have been made to revive the term for general usage (see, for example, Ted White's editorial in the May 1975 *Amazing*), but generally the word is now used in a purely historical sense.

SCIENTISM. "The uncritical acceptance of what is termed 'science' as objective knowledge, and a belief in the absolute value of what is called scientific," according to Gavin Browning, who also characterizes it as "the idea that human social problems can be solved by a development of 'science' and not by a resolution of social forces" [39]. Kingsley Amis uses the rather narrow definition of "the belief that any day now someone will discover a way of measuring human personality and society" and argues (as does Browning) that the belief is "rather widespread in science fiction" [8]. C. S. Lewis' definition, "less common among real scientists than among their readers," is "the belief that the supreme moral end is the perpetuation of our own species, and that this is to be pursued even if, in the process of being fitted for survival, our species has to be stripped of all those things for which we value it" [121]. In the more general sense of the belief that the only source of reliable knowledge lies in the inductive methods of science, scientism has often been evident in the work of Hard Science Fiction* writers, but is generally less commented on than the Antiscientism* that is also said to be evident in the genre. See also POSITIVISM.

SCI-FI. Neologism coined by science fiction fan Forrest J. Ackerman and which has become anathema to many science fiction writers and readers. Perhaps because of its widespread use in the popular media in what often seems a denigrating or stereotyping manner, "sci-fi" has, in effect, become science fiction's equivalent of "nigger." More recently, however, some writers and critics have begun to suggest that the term may in fact have a legitimate use in describing highly formulaic mass-audience entertainments, and in particular Hollywood movies. Isaac Asimov, for example, defines sci-fi as "trashy material sometimes confused, by ignorant people, with s.f." and cites the film *Godzilla Meets Mothra* as an example [14]. Damon Knight has suggested the term be used for "the crude, basic kind of s.f. that satisfies the appetite for pseudo-scientific marvels without appealing to any other portion of the intellect" (he also suggests the term be pronounced "skiffy") [111]. Somewhat less condemnatory, Elizabeth Anne Hull has suggested that films such as *Star Wars* might appropriately be termed sci-fi to distinguish them from the more complex (but still not clearly defined) fictions labeled SF.* Neither argument has gained much acceptance outside the science fiction community, however, and "sci-fi" remains in wide use as a popular media term for science fiction in general.

SECONDARY BELIEF. Belief in and acceptance of the Secondary World* of the fantasist or "sub-creator." Tolkien emphasizes that this is a more active kind of reader participation than that of Coleridge's Willing Suspension of Disbelief* [194].

SECONDARY UNIVERSE. Used by some critics, such as Franz Rottensteiner [163], as an alternative to Secondary World*; also the name of a series of early academic conferences on science fiction which began in 1968 and eventually led to the annual meetings of the Science Fiction Research Association.*

SECONDARY WORLD. The world created by the storyteller, according to Tolkien, with its own internal laws supporting Secondary Belief.* In practice, the term has attained a narrower meaning, and is often used to refer exclusively to the environments created by authors of High Fantasy* [194].

SECULAR ESCHATOLOGY. The treatment of eschatological themes in nonreligious contexts, as described by W. Warren Wagar. Most Cosmic Disaster Stories* in science fiction would belong in this tradition, which Wagar sees as representing a significant break in the development of western eschatological thought. His example of the first major work of fiction in this tradition is Mary Shelley's *The Last Man* (1826) [198].

SECULARIZATION. The appropriation of traditional religious beliefs or attitudes into more modern romantic or technological systems of thought. The concept is important to the study of science fiction and fantasy in that these literatures often employ cosmic or eschatological themes once characteristic only of religious texts. The term is suggested by W. Warren Wagar [198]. See also ESCHATOLOGICAL ROMANCE; SECULAR ESCHATOLOGY.

SEHNSUCHT. Literally, "longing," but used (principally by C. S. Lewis, although the term was familiar to George MacDonald) to refer to a specific variety of melancholic, romantic Desire* for "something that has never actually appeared in our experience" [122].

SEMIOTICS. An interdisciplinary study involving signs and sign functions. Sometimes formalized as a science and referred to as "semiology," the field was proposed by linguist Ferdinand de Saussure (1857–1913) and has been most fully developed within the context of linguistics. Through the influence of such critics as Roland Barthes, semiotics has also become a significant methodology in the analysis of literary texts, and has notably influenced a number of science fiction writers and critics, such as Samuel R. Delany, who has argued that the signifying process in fantastic literature is a key factor that sets it apart from Mundane* literature in its use of language [69].

SENSE OF WONDER. According to Darko Suvin, a "superannuated slogan of much SF criticism due for a deserved retirement into the same limbo as extrapolation" [187]. Nevertheless, the term remains a common, if perhaps unsatisfactory, attempt to describe the affective appeal of fantastic texts. See also WONDER.

SENTIMENTAL FANTASY. A rather vague term used by Diana Waggoner to describe fantastic works characterized by a "sickly, vapid air" [199].

SEQUEL. A work that continues a narrative begun in an earlier work, or portrays later events using the same characters. Arthur C. Clarke's *2010: Odyssey Two* (1982) is thus a sequel to his *2001: A Space Odyssey* (1968). Many authors prefer to make distinctions between sequels, Series,* and multivolume works such as trilogies. For example, the last two volumes of Tolkien's *Lord of the Rings* (1954–1955) were initially published as sequels to the first, but now the work is almost invariably referred to not as a novel with sequels, but as a three-volume novel. Frank Herbert's *Dune* series, on the other hand, contains some works that are sequels to others, and some that only share the general history and setting, while C. S. Lewis' "Narnia" tales were published in a different sequence from that implied by the internal chronology, making some of them sequels and some Prequels.*

SERIAL. A continuous narrative published in succeeding issues of a periodical, often with a number of regularly spaced dramatic climaxes at points determined by the length of each installment. While some early serial novels, such as the Penny Dreadfuls,* seemed designed to go on indefinitely with no immediate danger of book publication, serial stories in science fiction and fantasy Pulp* magazines were more often written in a limited number of installments. For a considerable period in the history of the genre, these magazine serials provided the major outlet for extended works of science fiction; many of them were in fact later published as novels. Some critics have therefore argued that certain characteristics of science fiction novels written between, roughly, 1926 and 1950 are in large part an outgrowth of the serial format. Among these characteristics are episodic structure, early and sometimes facile character development, and emphasis on frequent episodes of high action. See also FIX-UP.

SERIES. As opposed to a Serial,* a group of individual stories connected by common themes, settings, characters, or events. A few series, such as J. G. Ballard's Condensed Novels,* have only been connected by common structural or stylistic experiments. Individual stories in a series may range from short story to novel length, and some series (such as James Branch Cabell's *Biography of the Life of Manuel*, 1904–1929) have run to over twenty volumes. Others have provided the basis for works later published as single novels. (See Fix-Up.*) The series has been particularly attractive to writers of fantastic literature, perhaps because of an unwillingness to abandon a fully realized Secondary World* or science fiction environment. Samuel R. Delany has half-seriously suggested that the series may be "*the* basic form" of science fiction, and has gone on to argue that, despite chronological links among series stories, many series are in fact "successive approximations of some ideal-but-never-to-be-achieved-or-else-overshot structuring of themes, setting, characters." Delany regards this as evidence that the series provides authors with an unusual opportunity to explore simultaneous synchronic and diachronic structures within the same fictional field [70].

SF (S.F., S-F). Ambiguous abbreviation almost universally favored in the science fiction community over the more journalistic Sci-Fi,* but even less clearly defined. SF (or sf) is most often used as shorthand for science fiction, but has also been used for Science Fantasy,* Speculative Fiction,* or structural Fabulation.* Widely popularized even outside the science fiction community by Judith Merril in her series of "year's best" anthologies (1956–1969), all of which used the SF rubric, the usage has since become so prevalent that Isaac Asimov has suggested that "speculative fiction" may have been coined as an attempt to retain the initials SF while abandoning the more restrictive use of "science" as a modifier [14]. Some writers now prefer to use the term without specifying its particular meaning; if sci-fi is the "nigger" of the field, SF is its "Ms."

SHAGGY GOD STORY. Michael Moorcock's label for tales that seek to achieve a Sense of Wonder* by mechanically adapting biblical tales and providing science fictional "explanations" for them—as, for example, the "surprise ending" which reveals two characters to be Adam and Eve [144].

SHELF VELOCITY. See VELOCITY OF SALE.

SHILLING SHOCKER. Sometimes confused with the Penny Dreadfuls* of an earlier era, or the Dime Novels* popular in the United States about the same time, but generally referred to by collectors as short paperback novels, usually original, which gained popularity in England between 1880 and 1900, largely through sales at railway bookstalls. Less dependent upon debased gothicism than the earlier penny dreadfuls (though perhaps not greatly superior in style), these short novels (or short story collections) featured a number of science fiction–related titles and may have both influenced later authors and prepared later audiences. Among the science fiction titles that have been identified are Ritson Stewart's *The Professor's Last Experiment*, W. Grove's *A Mexican Mystery*, and Fergus Hume's *The Year of Miracle*.

SHORT NOVEL. A long story, but not quite long enough to warrant separate book publication. Rarely used by magazine editors in science fiction and fantasy (who sometimes preferred "complete novel" or Novella*), the term became popular among anthologists during the 1950s (compare Groff Conklin's *Six Great Short Novels of Science Fiction*, 1954; H. L. Gold's *Five Galaxy Short Novels*, 1958), although it was virtually interchangeable with "novelet." Conklin, in his anthology, argued that the short novel was ideally suited to the needs of science fiction, which often could not easily provide sufficient exposition within the short story length but which did not always require novel-length development for a single idea or concept. Conklin also defined the short novel length as 15–40,000 words, or approximately the length that magazine editors sometimes described as a novella.

SHORT SHORT STORY. Usually, a narrative of under 2,000 words. Often little more than a formalized joke or anecdote, the short short story in science fiction and fantasy is most often associated with humor and is often based on simple twists of familiar situations or themes. The most successful practitioner of the form may well have been Fredric Brown, some of whose stories have even entered Fandom* as science fiction jokes. A rather specialized form pioneered by Reginald Bretnor is sometimes known as the "Feghoot," from a series of stories written under the name "Grendel Briarton" for *The Magazine of Fantasy and Science Fiction*. The Feghoot is a story of usually only a few hundred words in which the goal is to construct a science fiction rationale for an egregious pun.

SHORT STORY. A narrative shorter than a Novella* but longer than a Short Short Story,* which by some accounts makes it a story of 2–15,000 words [93]. A short story has also been defined as "a depiction of one decisive experience in the protagonist's lifetime" by Algis Budrys, who characterized the early science fiction short story as heavily dependent on "structural tricks" such as surprise endings [43]. In this sense, the science fiction short story evolved initially from the plot-oriented tradition of O. Henry or Guy de Maupassant (whereas the somewhat less common fantasy short story often tended more toward the tale of "unified effect" pioneered by Edgar Allan Poe and Nathaniel Hawthorne). The influence of the realistic tradition of Chekhov and others entered science fiction in part through the influence of John W. Campbell, Jr., who was said to have demanded "realistic" stories in a fully realized science fiction environment. The modern tradition in the short story, identified with Katherine Mansfield, Ernest Hemingway, and others, did not become a major influence in fantastic literature until comparatively recently, but experimental or surrealistic forms have developed in fantastic literature side by side with their development in Mainstream* literature, a prime example being the work of Franz Kafka. Today, a mainstream short story author such as Donald Barthelme may use fantastic events or beings as readily as a science fiction author such as J. G. Ballard may use avant-garde narrative techniques.

SLICK MAGAZINE. Often used in opposition to Pulp* magazine in much the same way Mainstream* is used in opposition to science fiction. Slick magazines (so-called, presumably, because of the coated paper stock on which they were printed) were general-interest magazines such as *Collier's* or *The Saturday Evening Post* which printed fiction as well as a mix of popular articles, interviews, cartoons, and the like. Occasionally, beginning in the late 1940s, these magazines would publish science fiction or fantasy as well, and the ability of authors such as Ray Bradbury or Kurt Vonnegut, Jr., to place stories in them arguably had an influence on the general marketability of the genre and, indirectly, on stylistic and thematic developments as well. Within the magazine industry itself, "slicks" were positioned between the pulps, which appealed to broad but specialized audiences, and the "quality" magazines which appealed to the *literati*. Fiction in the slicks was generally regarded as reinforcing bourgeois values, whereas the "quality" magazines might challenge these values and the pulps exaggerated them.

SLUSHPILE. Editors' term for unsolicited stories or novels, usually by unknown writers and unmediated by agents or letters of inquiry.

SOCIAL FICTION. Historically associated with various movements of realism and social conscience in fiction, but given a particular definition by Isaac Asimov in his discussion of Social Science Fiction.* Asimov defined social fiction as a branch of literature that "moralizes about a current society through the device of dealing with a fictitious society" [35].

SOCIALIST REALISM. The Stalinist tenets for literature first suggested by Maxim Gorky and others at the 1934 Soviet Writers' Congress and more fully imposed in the late 1940s. The doctrine affected Soviet science fiction in some very direct ways. Science fiction subscribing to social realism was to extrapolate only slightly, if possible confining itself to applications of technology already under research. "Mysticism" or other effects sometimes characterized as the "sense of wonder" in western science fiction were often regarded as signs of "degeneracy" along with "formalism" or "cosmopolitanism," and could be grounds for condemnation of a writer or work [22].

SOCIAL SCIENCE FICTION. Ambiguous term (is "social" the modifier or is "social science"?) with two distinct usages: (1) Isaac Asimov, conceding that his definition of science fiction as a branch of literature "concerned with the impact of scientific advance upon human beings'' was perhaps too narrow for many tastes, argued that the definition only applied to a "subdivision" of the field which he called "social science fiction," "the only branch of science fiction that is sociologically significant" [35]. (2) A more common use of the term in the classroom treats "social science'" as the modifier and refers to works of science fiction that illustrate or illuminate particular problems or issues in the social sciences; see, for example, Willis McNelly and Leon Stover's anthology *Above the Human Landscape: A Social Science Fiction Anthology* (Goodyear, 1972).

SOCIOCULTURAL FANTASY. Works in which the principal fantastic element is a marvelous society or social organization, according to R. D. Mullen [141].

SOCIOLOGY DOMINANT. See ADVENTURE DOMINANT.

SOFT SCIENCE FICTION. Probably a back-formation from Hard Science Fiction,* and used sometimes to refer to science fiction based in the so-called soft sciences (anthropology, sociology, etc.), and sometimes to refer to science fiction in which there is little science or little awareness of science at all. Chad Oliver might be an example of an author who falls under the former definition, Ray Bradbury an example of the latter.

SOTERIOGRAPHY, SOTERIOLOGY. Soteriology is the branch of theology that deals with doctrines of divine salvation, soteriography texts associated with such beliefs. W. Warren Wagar has invoked these terms in his discussions of Eschatological* fiction [198], and Frederick A. Kreuziger has made the doctrines the basis of a study of science fiction [113].

SPACE FICTION. A term widely applied to science fiction by journalists and commentators from outside the genre, probably beginning in the 1950s and antedating Sci-Fi,* which to many writers and fans is only slightly less odious. Mark R. Hillegas, however, used the term as distinct from Cosmic Voyage* to refer to works set in outer space with little or no concern for the voyage there or back [54]. More recently, Doris Lessing has preferred this term for her ongoing series of connected science fiction novels *Canopus in Argos: Archives* (1979–1984).

SPACE OPERA. A term borrowed from Fandom,* where it was coined by Wilson Tucker in 1941 to refer to the "outworn spaceship yarn" of the sort that had been prevalent in the Pulps* during much of the 1930s [144]. Sometimes called adventure science fiction or Science Adventure,* space operas are generally fast-paced intergalactic adventures on a grand scale, most closely associated with E. E. Smith, Edmond Hamilton, and the early Jack Williamson.

Often characterized as a western in space or "straight fantasy in science fiction drag" (Norman Spinrad [34]), space opera may be either a historical or a generic term; contemporary films such as *Star Wars* have been labeled space operas, as have more complex works such as Cecilia Holland's 1976 novel *Floating Worlds*.

SPECIALIST MAGAZINE. A magazine that publishes a particular kind of fiction. While this might seem self-evident today, it meant a significant shift in the market for short popular fiction in the years following World War I, as general-interest Pulp* magazines such as those in the Munsey chain began to give way to magazines devoted especially to science fiction, horror, war stories, westerns, love stories, and the like. The development of the specialist magazines permitted the evolution of particular generic Protocols* which, at least in the case of science fiction, came increasingly to separate this fiction from the Mainstream*; eventually, of course, the specialist magazines became by far the dominant market for popular genre fiction, and as the general-interest pulps gave way to Slick Magazines,* genre authors found themselves increasingly isolated in a publishing Ghetto.* By the late 1940s, selling a story to a general-interest magazine meant, for many science fiction and fantasy writers, forgoing some of the assumptions about readership that had been developed during the pulp era.

SPECIALTY PRESS. Publishers who appeal to a specialized market. As American popular fantastic literature began to amass a body of work revered by fans but still largely ignored by book publishers, a number of fans undertook to preserve favorite works and authors by setting up publishing houses of their own devoted to particular kinds of fiction. The most prominent early example of this was Arkham House, founded by August Derleth and Donald Wandrei in 1939 primarily to preserve the work of H. P. Lovecraft, which otherwise was available only in ephemeral Pulps.* Following World War II, the specialty press became a significant force in the introduction of science fiction and fantasy to bookstores and libraries; other examples included Martin Greenberg and David A. Kyle's Gnome Press, Lloyd Arthur Eshbach's Fantasy Press, and Erle Korshak's Shasta Publishers. Following the discovery by general-interest publishers of a broader market for fantastic literature in the 1950s, many of these presses either failed or turned to publishing collectors' editions (as Phantasia Press currently does). Before the so-called academic awakening on the part of university presses and scholarly journals, these presses (such as Owlswick, Fantasy Press, and Advent) provided the only book-length works on science fiction and fantasy available, and many continue to publish such works.

SPECULATIVE FANTASY. Term suggested by Alexei Panshin to denote a "fictional form that uses removed worlds, characterized by distance and difference, as the setting for romantic-and-didactic narrative" [204].

SPECULATIVE FICTION. Alternative to "science fiction" preferred by a number of contemporary writers and possibly having a somewhat different meaning. Invited to contribute a piece to Lloyd Arthur Eshbach's 1947 symposium on science fiction writing *Of Other Worlds* [84], Robert A. Heinlein chose as his title "On the Writing of Speculative Fiction," and identified speculative fiction (a phrase he had used earlier, in an address to the 1941 World Science Fiction Convention) as a particular subtype of science fiction in which "established facts are extrapolated to produce a new situation, a new framework for human action." Heinlein commented that "we do not ordinarily mean this sort of story when we say 'science fiction,' " which at the time was still popularly associated with Space Opera.* Although Heinlein suggested the term as a general replacement for "science fiction" four years later at another World Science Fiction Convention, and although H. L. Gold that same year (1951) argued in an editorial in *Galaxy* that "speculation" rather than prediction ought to be a defining characteristic of science fiction [48], the term survived throughout the 1950s primarily as a description of a particular subtype of the genre, similar to what Isaac Asimov preferred to call Social Science Fiction.* In 1955, for example, Basil Davenport identified "speculative science fiction," based on social Extrapolation,* as distinct from both space operas and "scientific science fiction" [66]. As late as 1966, Judith Merril still defined it as a subtype, this time distinguishing it from "teaching stories" or "preaching stories" (Merril excluded "space adventure stories" from science fiction altogether), and defining it as "stories whose objective is to explore, to discover, to *learn*, by means of projection, extrapolation, analogue, hypothesis-and-paper-experimentation, something about the nature of the universe, of man, of 'reality' " [54].

By the late 1960s, however, a number of younger writers returned to Heinlein's 1951 suggestion that "speculative fiction" be adopted as a replacement term for "science fiction," or at least that science fiction be regarded as a subtype of speculative fiction rather than the other way round. Samuel R. Delany was among the first critics and writers to so use the term, which he characterized as being favored by writers who "have balked before the particular parameters Heinlein's s-f has established, primarily in the minds of editors, secondarily in the minds of other writers, and finally in the minds of readers" [70]. James Gunn added that these writers sought a term "to cover the various kinds of fiction that qualify under any reasonable definition but include no science," and one that signaled "a break with old pulp origins" [36].

Although the term has gained wide currency within the genre and has even regularly appeared in book titles (perhaps the first such usage was in Merril's

1968 anthology *England Swings SF: Stories of Speculative Fiction*), it has also generated some criticism from scholars and writers both. David Ketterer argues that the term "has been used somewhat confusedly" and blurs an important distinction between science fiction and fantasy [109]. Isaac Asimov more passionately objects to the term as an excuse for bad science fiction, "seized on by a number of people who know very little science and who feel more comfortable speculating freely and without having to raise a sweat by learning the rules of the game" [14]. These objections, however, are based on the very constraints that advocates of the term "speculative fiction" seek to overcome—the importance of generic boundaries (far more important to critics than to writers) and the "rules" of science fiction which purport to set limits on the way an author may imagine a work.

SPENGLERIAN. See HISTORICAL CYCLISM.

STATUS QUO SCIENCE FICTION. Frank Cioffi's term for that science fiction published in *Astounding* during the 1930s that introduces and resolves an anomaly within a recognizable social fabric, as opposed to subversive science fiction, in which the anomaly changes society, or Other World Science Fiction,* which is set entirely in an alternative world [52]. See also SUBVERSION.

STEAM LITERATURE. Applied in the 1830s and 1840s to cheap mass-market adventure tales; so called because of the recently developed rotary steam press on which such papers were printed. Although these "story papers" reprinted some earlier Gothic* fiction such as Edward Bulwer-Lytton's *Zanoni* (1842), they are perhaps most significant in that they directly led to the Dime Novel.*

STEF. Proposed around 1945 by a fan named Jack Speer and since used by almost no one except Algis Budrys in his 1980 essay "Paradise Charted" [43]. "Stef" is a neologism deriving from STF,* itself an abbreviation for Scientifiction,* and was apparently intended to provide a combinatory prefix as an alternative to such terms as "science fictional"; as Budrys says, the term is a "broad catchall" connoting fan activities and fannish attitudes.

STF. Abbreviation for Scientifiction,* and generally replaced by SF* when that term gave way to "science fiction."

STOCHASTIC FICTION. Boris Eizykman's term for the tendency of science fiction to work against its own mechanistic visions of the future by characteristically introducing unpredictable elements into the narrative. Science fiction thus becomes "the literature of alternate realities, using Chance, in the most effervescent of its drive-related aspects, to create fluid, experimental societies'' [78]. Examples of science fiction works that Eizykman cites are Philip K. Dick's *Solar Lottery* (1955) and Robert Silverberg's *The Stochastic Man* (1975).

STREET SCIENCE FICTION. Coined by Barry Malzberg [129] to describe (presumably) marketable popular science fiction primarily of the 1950s and 1960s. (The term ''says it all,'' according to Robert Bloch.) Malzberg later indicated the term was ''as opposed to Street & Smith'' science fiction, referring to the publisher of *Astounding Science Fiction* during this period.

STRONG TIME. See SACRED TIME.

STRUCTURAL FABULATION. See FABULATION.

STRUCTURALISM. Essentially a methodology whose use in literary scholarship derives from various techniques of segmenting phenomena into discrete parts and analyzing the relationships of those parts to each other and to larger structures. The major fields of structuralist thought that have contributed to these methods of analysis are linguistics (where the idea was pioneered by Ferdinand Saussure and later by Noam Chomsky), anthropology (where it is most closely associated with Claude Lévi-Strauss, whose analyses of mythic narratives have arguably had the greatest direct influence on the study of fantastic narratives), and psychology (where Jean Piaget and later Jacques Lacan developed methodologies used by later critics). Structuralist thought has influenced a number of critics of science fiction and fantasy, including Darko Suvin, Samuel R. Delany, Mark Rose, Robert Scholes, Eric S. Rabkin, and Christine Brooke-Rose.

STURGEON'S LAW. The principle that 90 percent of everything, including science fiction, is ''trash'' (or ''crud'' in the initial formulation). Theodore Sturgeon's often-quoted dictum, first delivered at a science fiction fan convention, reveals the common concern among science fiction writers that the genre is characteristically judged by its worst examples, and that fans sometimes overlook the fact that qualitative judgments need to be made within the field.

STYLE DOMINANT. See ADVENTURE DOMINANT.

SUB-CREATION. According to Tolkien, mythology and much fantasy is characterized by a fully realized Secondary World* which is the ''sub-creation'' of the author, or ''sub-creator'' [194].

SUBGENRE. A genre within a genre, or a group of works observing conventions more narrow than those imposed by the larger genre. Thus, Sword and Sorcery* would be a subgenre of fantasy. In some formulations, science fiction might be regarded as a subgenre of fantasy, or both science fiction and fantasy as subgenres of the larger Fantastic Romance.*

SUBJUNCTIVITY. "The tension on the thread of meaning that runs between sound-image and sound-image," according to Samuel R. Delany, who describes several "levels" of subjunctivity in fiction: "could have happened" (naturalistic fiction); "could not have happened" (fantasy); "have not happened" (science fiction and other "subcategories") [70]. See also NEGATIVE SUBJUNCTIVITY.

SUBLIME. Literally, "up to the threshold," and widely used to describe works of art or nature producing an effect of awe or reverence. Although in use in critical and aesthetic theory at least since the third-century philosopher Longinus, the notion of the "sublime" became of particular importance to the history of fantasy upon the publication of Edmund Burke's *A Philosophical Enquiry into the Origin of Our Idea of the Sublime and Beautiful* in 1757. Burke's argument that the sublime arose not out of beauty, but rather from an odd combination of feelings of terror and discomfort in the face of vastness, helped elevate the importance of the subjective ego in later discussions of art and provided a context both for the Gothic* novel and the Romantic movement. Kant and Schopenhauer refined the term, the latter associating it with will; and some later fantasy writers, notably David Lindsay, developed this notion to argue in favor of a deeper, more stark reality that might be approached through the fantastic. See also SACRAMENTALISM; WONDER.

SUBMYTH. According to Ursula K. Le Guin, "those images, figures, and motifs which have no religious or moral resonance and no intellectual or aesthetic value, but which are vigorously alive and powerful, so that they cannot be dismissed as mere stereotypes." Some of the examples Le Guin cites are the superman, the mad scientist, crazed computers, and the "blond heroes of Sword and Sorcery*" [115].

SUBTRACTIVE WORLD. A category of fantasy narratives characterized by Kathryn Hume as achieving their fantastic effect by omitting "large portions of human experience" or removing "expected material," such as logical causality. The subtractive world is thus made fantastic by virtue of what is left out, as opposed to Additive Worlds,* which introduce new and unexpected elements into the narrative world, or Contrastive Worlds,* which operate by contrast with the reader's experience [102].

SUBVERSION, SUBVERSIVE. Suggested by some critics as one of the principal social functions of fantastic literature. Rosemary Jackson and others have employed this term to describe the general relationship between the Desires* addressed by fantasy and the historical or cultural matrix of the work in question; fantasy becomes a "literature of subversion" insofar as it negates culturally dominant notions of reality and expresses unease or dissatisfaction with such notions [106]. A number of science fiction critics, however, have argued that fantasy and its related modes of the Gothic* have tended to be more conservative, and science fiction to be more "subversive." The chief arguments for this are that science fiction is characteristically postulated upon changes occurring in the "real" world (as opposed to the wholly alternative worlds of much fantasy), and that science fiction is not restricted to a consistent single moral vision. Sam Lundwall noted that as a young reader of science fiction, he found it to be offering "a subversive thing, the prospect of change"; Lundwall went on to speculate that this challenge to "the Establishment" may in part account for the marginal status often assigned to science fiction in terms of the Mainstream* [125]. Mark Rose elaborates the former point by observing that the impossibilities of fantasy reinforce one's sense of the real world through negation, whereas science fiction insists upon "the contingency of the present order of things" and is thus subversive where fantasy is conservative [160]. A similar point is made by Thomas H. Keeling in contrasting science fiction with the Gothic, which Keeling sees as riddled with anxieties concerning the past, the subconscious, and the prospect of change. Science fiction, on the other hand, "can be viewed as potentially 'subversive' insofar as it is not restricted to a moral vision of the world, and certainly not to a conventional Christian interpretation of reality" [181]. Such arguments almost inevitably depend upon theoretical considerations of genre more than upon examinations of particular works, and while advocates of the subversive nature of fantasy might have a hard time demonstrating that a work such as J. R. R. Tolkien's *The Hobbit* (1937) is subversive, so would the science fiction advocates find it difficult to demonstrate that the moral vision of an Isaac Asimov or a Robert Heinlein is especially revolutionary.

As a particular subtype, "subversive science fiction" is the label given by Frank Cioffi to those works in *Astounding* during the 1930s that went beyond the mere introduction and resolution of an anomaly or crisis in a recognizable social setting to depict anomalies that altered the nature of the society; he contrasts this with Status Quo Science Fiction* and Other World Science Fiction* [52].

SUPERGENRE. A broadly defined group of works ordinarily thought of as separate genres, but with some similar defining elements. Science fiction, fantasy, and horror, for example, may (according to R. D. Mullen) properly belong to the "supergenre" of Fantastic Romance* [141]. The term is employed in a similar sense by Eric S. Rabkin [156]. See also SUBGENRE.

SUPERNATURAL FICTION. Broadly, any fiction portraying events or figures that apparently violate natural laws. In practice, the term is usually confined to those works that make use of such conventional supernatural beliefs as ghosts, witches, demons, sorcery, etc. Many critics now prefer to exclude Secondary World* fantasy from this category, and associate it primarily with Low Fantasy.*

SUPERNATURAL SCIENCE. A term used by Dorothy Scarborough in her 1917 study *The Supernatural in Modern English Fiction* to describe authors such as Verne, Haggard, and Wells; as an early alternative to ''science fiction'' and as evidence of early attempts to subsume the genre into the tradition of supernatural writing, the term is of historical significance, but was not widely used.

SUPERSCIENCE. Although ''super science'' (or ''super-science'') was used in the title of two different magazines published in the 1940s and 1950s, the term itself is now used primarily to refer to 1930s fiction that predated the Campbell Era* but was not traditional Space Opera.* According to Algis Budrys, ''superscience'' was a genre magazine label in use from 1930 to 1938 to denote stories ''based on manipulations of frankly fictional physical phenomena'' [43]. Although often as melodramatic and overwritten as space operas, superscience stories focused upon increasingly extravagant ideas based loosely in popular physical science. See also THOUGHT-VARIANT.

SURREALISM. A movement in art and literature that gained its most prominent influence in Europe in the 1920s under the leadership of André Breton and that emphasized the role of the unconscious as a means of achieving artistic truth. The term has since come to be applied to a wide variety of works of fiction and art, including many fantasies that date from before and after the period of the movement's greatest notoriety. Among fantastic works of fiction deliberately associated with the movement is Robert M. Coates' *The Eater of Darkness* (1926). Although there have been a few attempts to appropriate the term in relation to science fiction and fantasy (Isaac Asimov suggested ''surrealistic fiction'' as a blanket term to cover both genres [14]), relatively little serious exploration has been attempted of the relationships between surrealism and modern fantastic literature, although David Ketterer has noted that the optimistic outlook of the surrealists together with their use of apocalyptic imagery and attempts to find expression for the objectified imagination provide substantial parallels with science fiction [109].

SWORD AND PLANET. Applied by Roger C. Schlobin and others to works that exhibit the conventions of Sword and Sorcery* fiction in a science fiction context; for example, by setting the events on a distant planet or using science

fiction conventions to "explain" such events [170]. See also SCIENCE
FANTASY.

SWORD AND SORCERY. Coined by Fritz Leiber in 1961 in response to
a request from novelist Michael Moorcock for a label for the Subgenre* in
which Moorcock worked, and since a standard term for a variety of violent
fantasy usually set in a primitive world and involving a superhuman (but not
supernatural) hero at odds with various wizards, witches, demons, spectres,
and warriors. Leiber himself was an early contributor to this subgenre, which
is most often associated with the "Conan" tales of Robert E. Howard (whose
own first story, "Spear and Fang," might well have provided another name
for the subgenre). Recently, a number of authors have expressed preference
for the more formal term Heroic Fantasy,* which L. Sprague de Camp has
defined as "stories laid in an imaginary world, superficially somewhat like
ours, but a world where magic works and machinery has not been invented"
(introduction to his anthology *The Spell of Seven*, New York: Pyramid, 1965).

SYMBOLIC FANTASY. Term used by Gary K. Wolfe to denote a genre
of fantasies characterized by a particular variety of Symbolism,* a transition
to an otherworldly setting, a conventional pattern of character groupings, a
quest motif, and a conscious dramatization of philosophical ideas. Examples
include George MacDonald, David Lindsay, and C. S. Lewis [210].

SYMBOLISM. A deliberate or formalized use of symbols or symbol patterns
in a literary work, or a movement associated with such usages. Apart from
its broad literary meaning and its association with literary movements of the
late nineteenth and early twentieth centuries, symbolism has taken on a rather
specific meaning for a number of fantasy writers, who often use the term to
distinguish their works from Allegory.* In particular, the use of this term by
authors such as George MacDonald, David Lindsay, and C. S. Lewis is almost
certainly influenced by Thomas Carlyle's observation in *Sartor Resartus* (1836)
that the symbol involves "some embodiment and revelation of the Infinite;
the Infinite is made to blend itself with the Finite, to stand visible, and as it
were, attainable there." MacDonald seemed to have a similar idea in mind
when he objected to reviews that treated his works as allegories, and Lindsay,
in his 1932 novel *Devil's Tor*, defined a symbol as "a mystic sign of the
Creator": "Whatever individual person or thing I paint [says Lindsay's artist]
must stand, not for itself, but for the entire scheme." Lewis, in his 1936
study *The Allegory of Love*, argued that while the allegorist leaves the given
to talk of "that which is confessedly less real," the symbolist "leaves the
given to find that which is more real . . . for the symbolist, it is we who are
the allegory" [119].

SYSTEMS MODEL. A schema for the study of science fiction suggested by Patricia Warrick, who defines a system as "an organized collection of related elements, characterized by a boundary and functional unity." Warrick argues that systems theory can be a useful critical approach to science fiction, particularly that which concerns cybernetics. She discusses works under the headings of "closed systems," inherited from classical mechanics and thermodynamics and revealed in dystopian fictions; "open systems," derived from biology and evolution and characteristic of science fiction stories of symbiosis and transformation (with examples by Arthur C. Clarke, Samuel R. Delany, and others); and "isolated systems," theoretical constructs for exploring hypothetical phenomena such as are characteristic of most early robot stories [201].

SYZYGY. Originally a poetic term referring to combining two metric feet as one or providing for the mellifluous flow from one word to the next in a poetic text. Theodore Sturgeon used the term in his fiction, however, to refer to idealized relationships involving both spiritual and physical union.

T

TALE OF THE FUTURE. Subgenre* of science fiction in which the depiction of a future world is central to the narrative. As Patrick Parrinder notes, this is often assumed to be "co-extensive with science fiction as a whole" [149]. A bibliography is I. F. Clarke's *The Tale of the Future* [55]. See also ANTICIPATION; CAUTIONARY TALE; EXTRAPO-LATION; FUTURE HISTORY.

TECHNOCRACY. Loosely employed to describe almost any imaginary society dominated by technicians and bureaucrats, whether it be dystopian (such as Kurt Vonnegut, Jr.'s *Player Piano*, 1952) or idealized (as in Hugo Gernsback's romances). Coined in 1919 by engineer William Henry Smyth as part of a serious proposal for such a government, the term later became associated with the ideas of Thorstein Veblen and applied to the concepts of Claude Henri de Saint-Simon. By the mid–1930s the movement gained popular interest under the name "Technocracy, Inc.," and apparently attracted some science fiction authors and fans, notably Nat Schachner (whose Technocracy-like "Revolt of the Scientists" series of stories appeared in *Wonder Stories* in 1933) and the young Ray Bradbury (who promoted the movement in his Fanzine* *Futuria Fantasia* in 1939–1940). With the rise of Nazism and criticisms of the movement as quasi-fascist, Technocracy's influence virtually disappeared during the war years, despite occasional discussions of technocratic ideas in the letter columns of magazines such as *Astounding* and the probable influence of Technocracy on part of science fiction Fandom* through the efforts of a fan named John B. Michel in the late 1930s and early 1940s. Today, the term is seldom used in its strictly historical sense in discussions of the genre.

TECHNOLOGICAL DETERMINISM. "The belief that man's future will be transformed by technological innovations whose impact it is impossible to predict," according to Patrick Parrinder, who cites this along with "evolutionism" as one of modern science fiction's "two basic rational methods of projecting the future" [181].

TECHNOLOGICAL UTOPIA. Kingsley Amis' description of a tradition begun by Jules Verne with *The Begum's Fortune* (1879) and continued in science fiction in narratives of societies—Utopian* or dystopian—whose economy and government is driven by advanced technology [8].

TECHNOPHILE. One who believes in the real or potential social benefits of technological progress, as opposed to a "technophobe" who fears technology. In common usage, John W. Campbell, Jr., would be an example of the former, Ray Bradbury of the latter. The term can become problematic in discussions of an author's body of work, however, since it can lead to oversimplifications and *ad hominem* arguments; thus, most authors resist either label. For example, Walter M. Miller, Jr., has been classified as "anti-technology" on the basis of his novel *A Canticle for Leibowitz* (1959), but David Samuelson has argued on the basis of his earlier work that he might more appropriately be regarded as a technophile suspicious of possible misuses of technology. Bradbury is a similar example; his "technophobe" image is to some extent belied by his enthusiastic nonfiction celebrations of the space program and other technological achievements.

TECHNOPHOBIA. Fear of technology. See also TECHNOPHILE.

TERMINAL FICTIONS. W. Warren Wagar's term for narratives concerned with last things—the end of the world, the destruction of civilizations, etc. [198]. See also ESCHATOLOGICAL ROMANCE.

TERROR. An emotional response to much Horror* and suspense fiction, sometimes used to describe a particular Subgenre* of such fiction. Ann Radcliffe ("On the Supernatural in Poetry," 1802) insisted upon a clear distinction between the emotions of terror and horror, arguing that terror, coming from without and associated with the Sublime,* "expands the soul," while horror arises from within and is associated with some sense of primal dread. Nevertheless, the "tale of terror" became virtually synonymous with the Gothic Novel* for much of literary history, in such works as Edith Birkhead's *The Tale of Terror: A Study of the Gothic Romance* (1921). Some authors have revived the term in recent years as distinct from "horror" to describe suspense or mystery stories, with or without supernatural elements, characterized by violence, pathological behavior, and victimization.

THEOLOGICAL ROMANCE. A novel that dramatizes theological arguments. C. S. Lewis once characterized his friend and colleague Charles Williams as a "romantic theologian"—"one who considers the theological implications of those experiences that are called romantic"— and the term "theological romance" thus emerged to describe the religiously oriented fantasies of Williams in particular and of Lewis, MacDonald, and others in general. The term was perhaps first used in this formal sense by W. R. Irwin [105].

THEORETICAL PLURALITY. The idea that scientific Paradigms* other than those currently accepted might provide the basis for science fiction. Samuel R. Delany identified this as the most notable characteristic of the critique of science—or popular conceptions of science—as developed by science fiction writers of the later 1930s, particularly those associated with John W. Campbell, Jr. In effect, "theoretical plurality" refers to challenging accepted scientific theory through fictional revisionism, particularly in regard to notions regarded as impossible (such as magic) or to practical limits imposed on phenomena by scientific theory. Hence, the common SF convention of faster-than-light travel is a pluralistic challenge to the aspect of relativity theory that declares such travel impossible [71].

THETIC. According to Jean-Paul Sartre, that mode of thought that might be formulated in propositions concerning the real or rational, whereas "nonthetic" refers to that which is unreal and not subject to such propositions. The French critic Irène Bessière used this distinction to identify the language of fantastic narratives as attempting to approach the nonthetic, but essentially propositional because of the limits upon language [106].

THOUGHT EXPERIMENT. (German, *Gedankenexperiment*). Term coined by physicist Werner Heisenberg to describe imaginary experiments under hypothetical ideal conditions in order to infer logically probable results. Of great importance in physics for most of the twentieth century, thought experiments have been invoked, in a somewhat looser definition (including social and technological change, for example), as a rationale for the intellectual significance of science fiction. "The science fiction writer," wrote Thomas M. Scortia, "is in the truest sense a professional fabricator of *gedankenexperimenten*" [36].

THOUGHT-VARIANT. A type of highly speculative science fiction adventure featured in *Astounding Stories* (later *Astounding Science Fiction*) during the 1930s. F. Orlin Tremaine assumed editorship of the magazine in October 1933, and in the November issue introduced a policy of including in each issue a "thought-variant" story concerning new concepts or controversial notions "without regard for the restrictions formerly placed upon this type of fiction." The first example was a time-travel story by Nat Schachner called "Ancestral Voices." As an early attempt to break free of the formulaic conventions and limitations of the genre and provide a market for a new kind of story, the idea had something in common with the later New Wave or Harlan Ellison's 1967 anthology *Dangerous Visions*; in practice, however, the policy generated relatively few significant stories. The most famous may be Murray Leinster's "Sidewise in Time" in the June 1934 issue, which was an early treatment of the Alternate World* theme.

TRIVALENCE. Samuel R. Delany's term for the characteristic nature of science fiction discourse. Science fiction, he argues, actually consists of three separate discourses: the "inward" discourse of characters, plot, and theme; the "outward" discourse of the imagined or created world; and the discourse of the "real world," which interacts with both. Since none of these discourses are ever quite congruent, "at best, the s-f writer harmonizes them" [69].

TRIVIALLITERATUR. See PARALITERATURE.

TWO CULTURES. C. P. Snow's formulation (in *The Two Cultures and the Scientific Revolution*, 1959) of an ongoing debate concerning the growing divergence between scientific and humanistic aspects of culture in the West. Earlier participants in the debate had included Thomas Henry Huxley, Matthew Arnold, H. G. Wells and Henry James, and Alfred North Whitehead. F. R. Leavis' response to Snow kept the debate alive well into the 1960s, when science fiction writers and scholars picked it up, usually arguing that those who most decried the schism were ignoring the literature that showed greatest promise of remedying it—namely, science fiction itself. See also ANTISCIENTISM; LUDDISM; SCIENTISM.

U

ULTRAISM. A literary movement founded in Madrid in 1919 and introduced to Argentina in 1921 by Jorge Luis Borges. Borges' version of *Ultráismo* involved a rejection of modernism, simplicity of style and narrative, and emphasis on metaphor and the combining of images; such ideas arguably exerted considerable influence on Borges' later fantastic work and thus indirectly on the development of the strong tradition of the fantastic in South American literature.

UNCANNY. Originally a Scottish word meaning mischievous or untrustworthy, eventually coming to mean weird or partaking of the supernatural. Modern critics, however, usually employ the term in more special meanings derived from Freud and Todorov. Freud, in his 1919 paper "The Uncanny," was actually discussing the German term *unheimlich* (literally, "unhomely") which he defined as a category of terrifying experience characterized by the re-emergence of something long-suppressed, such as the revival of infantile complexes or the apparent confirmation of primitive beliefs [91]. Todorov (influenced by Freud but not quite adopting his meaning of the term) characterized the uncanny simply as "the supernatural explained" (as in the novels of Ann Radcliffe) and contrasted it with the Marvelous,* or the supernatural accepted [193].

UNREAL. Not part of empirical reality. A number of critics, among them Christine Brooke-Rose, have argued that the traditional commonsense distinction between such reality and metaphysics (the "unreal") breaks down in the face of modern psychology, linguistics, and physics. As a result, the "unreal" becomes a matter of rhetorical strategy as much as philosophy, and fantastic literature emerges as a means of developing and testing such devices of language and rhetoric [38].

UR-SCIENCE FICTION. Brian Aldiss' term for early works, such as Lucian's *A True History* (ca. second century A.D.) or Swift's *Gulliver's Travels* (1729), which are sometimes cited as part of the history of science fiction [1]. See also PROTO SCIENCE FICTION.

UTOPIA. The genre that takes its name from Thomas More's 1516 work meaning "no place" in Greek (with a probable pun on "good place") and which according to some critics includes the Subgenres* of dystopia and Anti-Utopia.* Utopian fiction has evolved along substantially separate lines from modern generic fantasy and is more often associated with science fiction. Some critics have seen utopian elements in works as diverse as James Branch Cabell's Poictesme series (1904–1929) and J. R. R. Tolkien's *Lord of the Rings* (1954–1955), however, and it is apparent that utopian writers may make more or less use of fantasy techniques depending upon how their imaginary society is conceived. William Morris' *News from Nowhere* (1891), for example, makes use of much of the medievalism that characterized his fantasy romances, while George Orwell's *Animal Farm* (1945) places a dystopian narrative in the context of a Beast-Fable.* Science fiction is much more closely allied historically with utopian fiction, and often one is described as a subset of the other. "Utopia" has been defined as any transcending of human boundaries (Ernest Bloch) or as transcending reality and social orders (as opposed to "ideology," in the work of Karl Mannheim), but it is most often defined as a fictional narrative whose central theme is an imaginary state or community, sometimes with the corollary that such a state should be idealized or that it should contain an implied critique of an existing society or societies. Darko Suvin has argued that the imaginary community of a utopia must be "organized according to a more perfect principle than in the author's community" and that a utopia is "based on estrangement arising out of an alternative historical hypothesis" [187].

V

VELOCITY OF SALE. The number of copies of a book sold during a given period (some book retailers use the more surrealistic term "shelf velocity"), often based on extraordinarily detailed computer records maintained on a weekly or even daily basis. Such concepts are used by some publishers and booksellers as a way of determining print orders, reprints, remaindering, and other factors affecting a book's commercial availability. This practice probably has considerable impact on the teaching of fantastic literature and possibly even on the nature of science fiction and fantasy itself, since the velocity of sale of a particular title is apt to determine whether that title is available for classroom teaching, and since publishers are influenced to seek books with a short but "high-velocity" shelf life as opposed to Mid-List* titles which might enjoy a slower but persistent sales pattern.

VERNIAN. Fiction that, in the tradition of Jules Verne, focuses on technological extrapolation within the context of "accepting the status quo of the system in power," according to Donald A. Wollheim. Wollheim has divided the principal traditions of science fiction into what he calls "Vernian" and "Wellsian," the latter concerned with the impact of scientific change upon social institutions and relations [212].

VISIONARY LITERATURE. A rather loosely used term that may refer to heightened, transforming perceptions (as with the Romantic poets); to literature conceived and presented as prophecy or revelation (as with Blake or Dante); to medieval dream visions (as with *Piers Ploughman*); or—perhaps most commonly in regard to modern fantasy—to works whose fantastic beings, settings, or events seem of great symbolic significance but cannot readily be described as allegories, pastiches, or homages to traditional forms such as the epic. The term also sometimes refers to modern works that partake of any of the above definitions or seem to encode substantial unconscious content. The late novels of Philip K. Dick are examples of works deriving from the science fiction tradition which also partake of more traditional meanings of this term.

VOLKSMÄRCHEN. A traditional, or folk, Märchen,* as distinguished from the literary Fairy Tale* or Kunstmärchen.*

VOR-SCHEIN. See ANTICIPATORY ILLUSION.

VOYAGES EXTRAORDINAIRES. "Extraordinary journeys," the term that the publisher Hetzel used to describe a long series of novels by Jules Verne which began with *Five Weeks in a Balloon* (1863). Subtitled "Known and 'Unknown Worlds," the series dominated the remainder of Verne's career and included most of his best-known science fiction; although usually confined to Verne, the term also represents a historical connection between modern science fiction and the Imaginary Voyage* tradition popular in earlier fiction. In fact, the term had been used well before Verne, and first gained prominence in 1735, with the publication of Charles de F. Mouhy's *Lamekis*, which was subtitled *les voyages extraordinaires d'un Egyptien dans la terre intérieure*. Later commentators used the term as a particular subtype of the imaginary voyage and, interestingly, a type that was not necessarily fantastic but concerned travel to real but little-known lands [95]. Under this scheme, Verne's works would be classified as "fantastic voyages." (See Geoffroy Atkinson, *The Extraordinary Voyage in French Literature*, 1920, 1922.)

W

WEIRD TALE. Very loosely used term, most often referring to Uncanny* or Occult Fiction,* but in recent decades (thanks to the influence of the Pulp* magazine *Weird Tales*) often used specifically to denote Horror* stories.

WELLSIAN. See VERNIAN.

WHIMSY. Originally, lightheadedness or vertigo, but widely used to mean any writing of an eccentric or lightly humorous nature. The term has on occasion been used to describe playful fantasies; examples might include such authors as Hope Mirrlees or, more recently, James P. Blaylock.

WILLING SUSPENSION OF DISBELIEF. The most often quoted phrase from Samuel Taylor Coleridge's *Biographia Literaria* (1817). The phrase originated in Coleridge's description of his intention in his earlier *Lyrical Ballads* (1798) to deal with supernatural or romantic figures, but "to procure for these shadows of imagination that willing suspension of disbelief for the moment, which constitutes poetic faith." The term has often been cited as a necessary rhetorical strategy for fantastic narratives, but some fantasy writers themselves, notably J. R. R. Tolkien, have objected to this usage, arguing that it implies a more passive condition on the part of the reader than that of the Secondary Belief* of true fantasy [194].

WONDER. Frequently invoked in definitions of fantasy but seldom defined, as in C. N. Manlove's phrase "a fiction evoking wonder" [132]. The term is equally common in discussions of science fiction, with its

"Sense of Wonder,"* but it is quite possible the meaning there is somewhat different, relating to philosophical notions of the undiscovered universe and romantic notions of the Sublime* in the face of vastness. In fantasy, the term need not imply awe and terror in the face of the natural world, but rather suggests the Desire* and longing arising out of the promise of other worlds or states of being. In this sense, the term is perhaps related to *Sehnsucht*.* Casey Fredericks has characterized the "wonder effect" as "presenting both a radical and a recognizable change on the known world" [89]. As for the science-fictional "sense of wonder," Samuel R. Delany has suggested that the phrase gained currency through the criticism of Damon Knight, and may have been borrowed from W. H. Auden's 1939 poem "In Memory of Sigmund Freud" (which spoke of the "sense of wonder" offered by the night) [72]. It is equally possible, however, that the phrase had gained some currency before the Auden poem, perhaps through the use of "wonder" in the titles of Pulp* magazines as early as 1929.

WONDER TALE. Sometimes used as a translation of Märchen,* sometimes to refer indiscriminately to Fairy Tales,* and sometimes to refer only to fairy and folk tales with marvelous or supernatural occurrences.

WORLD-MAKING. Lin Carter's term for the creation of imaginary worlds as the background for fantasy narratives; see Secondary World* [47]. For a science fiction equivalent, see Planet-Building.*

Y

YELLOWBACK. Popular fiction, bound in paper-covered boards and popular during the late nineteenth and early twentieth centuries in England. Somewhat more expensive than Shilling Shockers* and often reprints, yellowbacks occasionally featured works of fantastic literature, such as Edwin Arnold's *Phra the Phoenician* (1890).

YOUNG ADULT. See JUVENILE.

Z

ZERO WORLD. The "real world"; more specifically, the world of "empirically verifiable properties around the author," according to Darko Suvin. This "naturalistic" world is used to describe the central reference point from which various genres of fantastic and realistic literature may be located [187]. See also CONSENSUS REALITY.

Works Consulted

1. Aldiss, Brian W. *Billion Year Spree: The True History of Science Fiction*. Garden City, N.Y.: Doubleday, 1973.

2. ———. *This World and Nearer Ones: Essays Exploring the Familiar*. London: Weidenfeld & Nicolson, 1978.

3. Alexander, Lloyd. "Wishful Thinking—or Hopeful Dreaming?" *The Horn Book Magazine* 44 (August 1968): 383–390. (Reprinted in Boyer and Zahorski, [29].)

4. Allen, Dick, ed. *Science Fiction: The Future*. New York: Harcourt, Brace, Jovanovich, 1971.

5. ———, and Lori Allen, ed. *Looking Ahead: The Vision of Science Fiction*. New York: Harcourt, Brace, Jovanovich, 1975.

6. Allen, L. David. *Science Fiction Reader's Guide*. Lincoln, Neb.: Centennial Press, 1974.

7. Alpers, Hans Joachim. "Loincloth, Double Ax, and Magic: 'Heroic Fantasy' and Related Genres." trans. Robert Plank. *Science Fiction Studies* 14 (March 1978): 19–32.

8. Amis, Kingsley. *New Maps of Hell*. New York: Ballantine, 1960.

9. Angenot, Marc. "The Absent Paradigm." *Science Fiction Studies* 17 (March 1979): 9–19.

10. ———, and Nadia Khouri. "An International Bibliography of Prehistoric Fiction." *Science Fiction Studies* 23 (March 1981): 38–53.

11. Apter, T. E. *Fantasy Literature: An Approach to Reality*. Bloomington: Indiana University Press, 1982.

12. Ash, Brian, ed. *The Visual Encyclopedia of Science Fiction*. New York: Harmony Books, 1977.

13. Ashley, Michael, ed. *The History of the Science Fiction Magazine*, 4 vols. London: New English Library, 1974–1978.

14. Asimov, Isaac. *Asimov on Science Fiction*. Garden City, N.Y.: Doubleday, 1981.

15. Atheling, William, Jr. [James Blish]. *The Issue at Hand: Studies in Contemporary Magazine Science Fiction*. Chicago: Advent, 1964.

16. ———. *More Issues at Hand: Critical Studies in Contemporary Science Fiction*. Chicago: Advent, 1970.

17. Attebery, Brian. *The Fantasy Tradition in American Literature: From Irving to Le Guin*. Bloomington: Indiana University Press, 1980.

18. ———. "Science Fantasy," in Cowart and Wymer [63].

19. Bailey, J. O. *Pilgrims through Space and Time: Trends and Patterns in Scientific and Utopian Fiction*. New York: Argus Books, 1947.

20. Baker, Robert A., and Michael T. Nietzel. "The Science Fiction Detective Story: Tomorrow's Private Eyes." *The Armchair Detective* 18, no. 2 (Spring 1985): 140–150.

21. Barnes, Myra Edward. *Linguistics and Languages in Science Fiction*. New York: Arno, 1974.

22. Barron, Neil, ed. *Anatomy of Wonder: An Historical Survey and Critical Guide to the Best of Science Fiction*, 2d ed. New York: R. R. Bowker, 1981.

23. Barth, Melissa Ellen. "Problems in Generic Classification: Toward a Definition of Fantasy Fiction." *DAI* 42 (1981): 2125A.

24. Berger, Harold L. *Science Fiction and the New Dark Age*. Bowling Green, Ohio: Popular Press, 1976.

25. Berman, Ruth. "Critical Reactions to Fantasy in Four Nineteenth-Century Periodicals: *Edinburgh Review*, *Blackwood's*, *Fraser's*, and *Cornhill*." *The Sphinx* 4, no. 13 (1981): 1–37.

26. Bettelheim, Bruno. *The Uses of Enchantment: The Meaning and Importance of Fairy Tales*. New York: Alfred A. Knopf, 1976.

27. Bleiler, Everett F., ed. *The Guide to Supernatural Fiction*. Kent, Ohio: Kent State University Press, 1983.

28. Blish, James. "Introduction." *The Light Fantastic: Science Fiction Classics from the Mainstream*, ed. Harry Harrison. New York: Scribner's, 1971. (See also Atheling, William, Jr.)

29. Boyer, Robert H., and Kenneth J. Zahorski. *Fantasists on Fantasy: A Collection of Critical Reflections*. New York: Avon, 1984.

30. ———. "Introduction." *Dark Imaginings: A Collection of Gothic Fantasy*. New York: Dell, 1978.

31. ———. "Introduction." *The Fantastic Imagination: An Anthology of High Fantasy*. New York: Avon, 1977.

32. ———. "Introduction." *The Fantastic Imagination II: An Anthology of High Fantasy*. New York: Avon, 1978.

33. ———. "Introduction." *Visions of Wonder: An Anthology of Christian Fantasy*. New York: Avon, 1981.

34. Bretnor, Reginald, ed. *The Craft of Science Fiction*. New York: Harper & Row, 1976.

35. ———, ed. *Modern Science Fiction: Its Meaning and Its Future*. New York: Coward-McCann, 1953.

36. ———, ed. *Science Fiction Today and Tomorrow*. New York: Harper and Row, 1974.

37. Briggs, Julia. *Night Visitors: The Rise and Fall of the English Ghost Story*. London: Faber and Faber, 1977.

38. Brooke-Rose, Christine. *A Rhetoric of the Unreal: Studies in Narrative and Structure, Especially of the Fantastic*. Cambridge, Mass.: Cambridge University Press, 1981.

39. Browning, Gavin. "Scientism in Science Fiction." *Science-Fiction Studies* 33 (Spring 1985): 24–35.

40. Budrys, Algis. *Benchmarks: Galaxy Bookshelf*. Carbondale: Southern Illinois University Press, 1985.

41. ———. "Literatures of Milieux." *Science Fiction Studies* 31 (July 1984): 5–17.

42. ———. "On Writing." *Locus*, 11, no. 2 (March 1978): 4–6.

43. ———. "Paradise Charted." *Triquarterly* 49 (Fall 1980): 5–75.

44. Bullock, Alan, and Oliver Stallybrass, eds. *The Harper Dictionary of Modern Thought*. New York: Harper, 1977.

45. Campbell, Joseph. *The Hero with a Thousand Faces*. Bollingen Series XVII. Princeton, N.J.: Princeton University Press, 1949.

46. Canary, Robert H. "Science Fiction as Fictive History." *Extrapolation* 16 (December 1974): 81–95.

47. Carter, Lin. *Imaginary Worlds: The Art of Fantasy*. New York: Ballantine, 1973.

48. Carter, Paul. *The Creation of Tomorrow: Fifty Years of Magazine Science Fiction*. New York: Columbia University Press, 1977.

49. Cawelti, John. *Adventure, Mystery, and Romance: Formula Stories as Art and Popular Culture*. Chicago: University of Chicago Press, 1976.

50. Chesterton, G. K. "The Ethics of Elfland." *Orthodoxy*. New York: Dodd, Mead, 1908.

51. ———. "Fairy Tales," in Boyer and Zahorski [29].

52. Cioffi, Frank. *Formula Fiction? An Anatomy of American Science Fiction, 1930–1940*. Westport, Conn.: Greenwood Press, 1982.

53. Clareson, Thomas D., ed. *Many Futures, Many Worlds: Theme and Form in Science Fiction*. Kent, Ohio: Kent State University Press, 1977.

54. ———, ed. *SF: The Other Side of Realism*. Bowling Green, Ohio: Bowling Green University Popular Press, 1971.

55. Clarke, I. F. *Tale of the Future from the Beginning to the Present Day: An Annotated Bibliography*, 3d ed. London: Library Association, 1978.

56. ———. *Voices Prophesying War, 1763–1984*. Oxford: Oxford University Press, 1966.

57. Clayton, David. "On Realistic and Fantastic Discourse," in Slusser, Rabkin, and Scholes [180].

58. Clute, John. "Posthumous Fantasy," in Magill [127], Vol. 5, pp. 2383–2890.

59. Cogell, Elizabeth Cummins. "The Middle Landscape Myth in Science Fiction." *Science Fiction Studies* 15 (July 1978): 134–142.

60. Conklin, Groff. "Introduction." *The Best of Science Fiction*. New York: Crown, 1946.

61. ———. "Introduction." *Six Great Short Novels of Science Fiction*. New York: Dell, 1954.

62. Cott, Jonathan. "Notes on Fairy Faith and the Idea of Childhood." *Beyond the Looking Glass: Extraordinary Works of Fantasy and Fairy Tale*, ed. Jonathan Cott. New York: Stonehill, 1973.

63. Cowart, David, and Thomas L. Wymer, eds. *Twentieth Century American Science Fiction Writers. Dictionary of Literary Biography*, vol. 8, parts 1 and 2. Detroit: Gale Research, 1981.

64. Crossley, Robert. "Education and Fantasy." *College English* 37 (1975): 281–293.

65. ———. "Pure and Applied Fantasy, or From Faerie to Utopia," in Schlobin [171].

66. Davenport, Basil. *Inquiry into Science Fiction*. New York: Longmans, Green, 1955.

67. ———, Robert A. Heinlein, C. M. Kornbluth, Alfred Bester, and Robert Bloch. *The Science Fiction Novel: Imagination and Social Criticism*. Chicago: Advent, 1959.

68. de Camp, L. Sprague, and Catherine C. de Camp. *Science Fiction Handbook, Revised*. Philadelphia: Owlswick, 1975.

69. Delany, Samuel R. *The American Shore*. Elizabethtown, N.Y.: Dragon Press, 1978.

70. ———. *The Jewel-Hinged Jaw: Notes on the Language of Science Fiction*. New York: Berkley, 1977.

71. ———. "Reflections on Historical Models of Modern English Language Science Fiction." *Science Fiction Studies* 21 (July 1980): 135–149.

72. ———. "Some Reflections on SF Criticism." *Science Fiction Studies* 25 (November 1981): 233–239.

73. ———. *Starboard Wine: More Notes on the Language of Science Fiction*. Elizabethtown, N.Y.: Dragon Press, 1984.

74. Del Rey, Lester. *The World of Science Fiction: 1926–1976: The History of a Subculture*. New York: Ballantine, 1979.

75. Disch, Thomas M. "Books." *The Magazine of Fantasy and Science Fiction* 60 (February 1981): 40–47.

76. Duffy, Maureen. *The Erotic World of Faery*. London: Hodder and Stoughton, 1972.

77. Eagleton, Terry. *Literary Theory: An Introduction*. Minneapolis: University of Minnesota Press, 1983.

78. Eizykman, Boris. "Chance and Science Fiction: SF as Stochastic Fiction." trans. Will Straw. *Science Fiction Studies* 29 (March 1983): 24–34.

79. Eliade, Mircea. *Myths, Dreams and Mysteries: The Encounter between Contemporary Faiths and Archaic Realities*. trans. Philip Mairet. New York: Harper & Row, 1960.

80. Elgin, Don D. *The Comedy of the Fantastic: Ecological Perspectives on the Fantasy Novel*. Westport, Conn.: Greenwood Press, 1985.

81. Elkins, Charles. "Science Fiction versus Futurology: Dramatic versus Rational Models." *Science Fiction Studies* 17 (March 1979): 20–31.

82. Erlich, Richard, and Thomas P. Dunn, eds. *Clockwork Worlds: Mechanized Environments in Science Fiction*. Westport, Conn.: Greenwood Press, 1983.

83. ———, eds. *The Mechanical God: Machines in Science Fiction*. Westport, Conn.: Greenwood Press, 1982.

84. Eshbach, Lloyd Arthur, ed. *Of Worlds Beyond: The Science of Science Fiction Writing*. Reading, Penn.: Fantasy Press, 1947.

85. Fiedler, Leslie. "Introduction." *Beyond the Looking Glass: Extraordinary Works of Fantasy and Fairy Tale*, ed. Jonathan Cott. New York: Stonehill, 1973.

86. ———. *Love and Death in the American Novel*. New York: Criterion, 1960.

87. Forster, E. M. *Aspects of the Novel*. New York: Harcourt, Brace, & World, 1927.

88. Franklin, H. Bruce, ed. *Future Perfect: American Science Fiction of the Nineteenth Century*. New York: Oxford University Press, 1966.

89. Fredericks, Casey. *The Future of Eternity: Mythologies of Science Fiction and Fantasy*. Bloomington: Indiana University Press, 1982.

90. ———. "Problems of Fantasy." *Science Fiction Studies* 5 (1978): 33–44.

91. Freud, Sigmund. "The Uncanny." *Complete Psychological Works*. ed. and trans. James Strachey, Vol. 17, pp. 217–252. London: Hogarth Press, 1953.

92. Frye, Northrop. *Anatomy of Criticism: Four Essays*. Princeton, N.J.: Princeton University Press, 1957.

93. ———, Sheridan Baker, and George Perkins. *The Harper Handbook to Literature*. New York: Harper & Row, 1985.

94. Gerber, Richard. *Utopian Fantasy: A Study of English Utopian Fiction since the End of the Nineteenth Century*. London: Routledge & Kegan Paul, 1955.

95. Gove, Philip Babcock. *The Imaginary Voyage in Prose Fiction*. New York: Columbia University Press, 1941.

96. Griffin, Brian, and David Wingrove. *Apertures: A Study of the Writings of Brian Aldiss*. Contributions to the Study of Science Fiction and Fantasy No. 8. Westport, Conn.: Greenwood Press, 1984.

97. Gunn, James. *Alternate Worlds: The Illustrated History of Science Fiction.* Englewood Cliffs, N.J.: Prentice-Hall, 1975.

98. Haase, Donald P. "Romantic Theory of the Fantastic," in Magill [127], Vol. 5, pp. 2247–2258.

99. Hartwell, David. *Age of Wonders: Exploring the World of Science Fiction.* New York: Walker, 1984.

100. Hassler, Donald M. *Comic Tones in Science Fiction: The Art of Compromise with Nature.* Westport, Conn.: Greenwood Press, 1982.

101. Hienger, Jörg. "The Uncanny in Science Fiction." trans. Elsa Schieder. *Science Fiction Studies* 18 (July 1979): 144–152.

102. Hume, Kathryn. *Fantasy and Mimesis: Responses to Reality in Western Literature.* New York: Methuen, 1984.

103. Hunter, Mollie. "One World." *Horn Book Magazine* 51 (1975): 557–563, and 52 (1976): 32–38. (Reprinted in Boyer and Zahorski [29].)

104. Huntington, John. *The Logic of Fantasy: H. G. Wells and Science Fiction.* New York: Columbia University Press, 1982.

105. Irwin, W. R. *The Game of the Impossible: A Rhetoric of Fantasy.* Urbana: University of Illinois Press, 1976.

106. Jackson, Rosemary. *Fantasy: The Literature of Subversion.* London: Methuen, 1981.

107. Kayser, Wolfgang. *The Grotesque in Art and Literature.* trans. U. Weisstein. Bloomington: Indiana University Press, 1963.

108. Ketterer, David. *New Worlds for Old: The Apocalyptic Imagination, Science Fiction, and American Literature.* Bloomington: Indiana University Press, 1974.

109. ———. "Science Fiction and Allied Literature." *Science Fiction Studies* 3, no. 8 (March 1976): 64–75.

110. Knight, Damon. *In Search of Wonder: Essays on Modern Science Fiction,* 2d ed. Chicago: Advent, 1967.

111. ———, ed. *Turning Points: Essays on the Art of Science Fiction.* New York: Harper & Row, 1977.

112. Krappe, Alexander H. *The Science of Folklore.* New York: Norton, 1964 [1929].

113. Kreuziger, Frederick A. *Apocalypse and Science Fiction: A Dialectic of Religious and Secular Soteriologies.* Chico, Calif.: Scholars Press, 1982.

114. Le Guin, Ursula K. "Foreword." *The Wind's Twelve Quarters.* New York: Harper & Row, 1975.

115. ———. *The Language of the Night.* ed. Susan Wood. New York: Putnam's, 1978. ("Dreams Must Explain Themselves" and "From Elfland to Poughkeepsie" reprinted in Boyer and Zahorski [29].)

116. Lem, Stanislaw. "Metafantasia: The Possibilities of SF." trans. Etelka de Laczay and Istvan Csicsery-Ronay. *Science Fiction Studies* 23 (March 1981): 54–71.

117. ———. *Microworlds: Writings on Science Fiction and Fantasy.* New York: Harcourt Brace Jovanovich, 1985.

118. Lerner, Frederick Andrew. *Modern Science Fiction and the American Literary Community*. Metuchen, N.J.: Scarecrow Press, 1985.

119. Lewis, C. S. *Allegory of Love: A Study in Medieval Tradition*. Oxford: Oxford University Press, 1936.

120. ———. *An Experiment in Criticism*. Cambridge, Mass.: Cambridge University Press, 1965.

121. ———. *Of Other Worlds: Essays and Stories*. ed. Walter Hooper. New York: Harcourt Brace, & World, 1966.

122. ———. *The Weight of Glory and Other Addresses*. New York: Macmillan, 1949.

123. Lochhead, Marion. *Renaissance of Wonder: The Fantasy Worlds of C. S. Lewis, J. R. R. Tolkien, George MacDonald, E. Nesbit and Others*. New York: Harper & Row, 1977.

124. Lovecraft, H. P. *Supernatural Horror in Literature*. New York: Abramson, 1945. (Originally written in 1927; reprinted by Dover, New York, in 1973.)

125. Lundwall, Sam. *Science Fiction: What It's All About*. New York: Ace, 1971.

126. MacDonald, George. "The Fantastic Imagination." *The Gifts of the Child Christ: Fairy Tales and Stories for the Childlike*. ed. Glenn Edward Sadler. Grand Rapids, Mich.: William B. Eerdmans, 1973. Vol. 1, pp. 23–28.

127. Magill, Frank, ed. *Survey of Modern Fantasy Literature*. 5 vols. Englewood Cliffs, N.J.: Salem Press, 1983.

128. ———, ed. *Survey of Science Fiction Literature*. 5 vols. Englewood Cliffs, N.J.: Salem Press, 1979.

129. Malzberg, Barry. *The Engines of the Night: Science Fiction in the Eighties*. New York: Harper, 1982.

130. Manguel, Alberto. "Foreword." *Black Water: The Book of Fantastic Literature*. New York: Clarkson N. Potter, 1983.

131. Manlove, C. N. *The Impulse of Fantasy Literature*. Kent, Ohio: Kent State University Press, 1983.

132. ———. *Modern Fantasy: Five Studies*. Cambridge, Mass.: Cambridge University Press, 1975.

133. Meyers, Walter E. *Aliens and Linguists: Language Study and Science Fiction*. Athens: University of Georgia Press, 1980.

134. Mobley, Jane. "Toward a Definition of Fantasy Fiction." *Extrapolation* 15 (1974): 117–128.

135. ———, ed. *Phantasmagoria: Tales of Fantasy and the Supernatural*. New York: Anchor, 1977.

136. Molson, Francis J. "Ethical Fantasy for Children," in Schlobin [171].

137. Moorman, Charles. *Arthurian Triptych*. Berkeley: University of California Press, 1960.

138. Moskowitz, Sam. *Explorers of the Infinite: Shapers of Science Fiction*. Cleveland: World, 1963.

139. ———. *Seekers of Tomorrow: Masters of Modern Science Fiction*. Cleveland: World, 1965.

140. ———. *Strange Horizons: The Spectrum of Science Fiction*. New York: Scribner's, 1976.

141. Mullen, R. D. "Books in Review: Supernatural, Pseudonatural, and Sociocultural Fantasy." *Science Fiction Studies* no. 16 (November 1978): 291–298.

142. Nicholls, Peter, ed. *Science Fiction at Large*. London: Gollancz, 1976.

143. ———. "Science Fiction and the Mainstream, Part 2: The Great Tradition of Proto Science Fiction." *Foundation* 5 (January 1974): 9–43.

144. ———, ed. *The Science Fiction Encyclopedia*. Garden City, N.Y.: Doubleday, 1979.

145. Nicolson, Marjorie Hope. *Voyages to the Moon*. New York: Macmillan, 1948.

146. Pagetti, Carlo. "*The First Men in the Moon*: H. G. Wells and the Fictional Strategy of his 'Scientific Romances.' " trans. Marie-Christine Hubert. *Science Fiction Studies* 21 (July 1980): 124–134.

147. Panshin, Alexei and Cory. "Science Fiction and the Dimension of Myth." *Extrapolation* 22 (1981): 127–139.

148. ———. *SF in Dimension: A Book of Explorations*. Chicago: Advent, 1976.

149. Parrinder, Patrick. *Science Fiction: Its Criticism and Teaching*. London: Methuen, 1980.

150. Philmus, Robert M. *Into the Unknown: The Evolution of Science Fiction from Francis Godwin to H. G. Wells*. Berkeley: University of California Press, 1970.

151. Plank, Robert. *The Emotional Significance of Imaginary Beings: A Study of the Interaction between Psychopathology, Literature, and Reality in the Modern World*. Springfield, Ill.: Charles C. Thomas, 1968.

152. Pohl, Frederik. "The Game-Playing Literature." in *Clarion: An Anthology of Speculative Fiction and Criticism from the Clarion Writers' Workshop*. ed. Robin Scott Wilson. New York: New American Library, 1971, pp. 72–75.

153. Prickett, Stephen. "Religious Fantasy in the Nineteenth Century," in Magill [127], vol 5, pp. 2369–2382.

154. ———. *Victorian Fantasy*. Bloomington: University of Indiana Press, 1979.

155. Propp, Vladimir. *Morphology of the Folktale*. trans. Laurence Scott. Austin: University of Texas Press, 1968.

156. Rabkin, Eric S. *The Fantastic in Literature*. Princeton, N.J.: Princeton University Press, 1976.

157. ———, ed. *Fantastic Worlds: Myths, Tales, and Stories*. New York: Oxford University Press, 1979.

158. ———, Martin H. Greenberg, and Joseph D. Olander, eds. *The End of the World*. Carbondale: Southern Illinois University Press, 1983.

159. Read, Herbert. *English Prose Style*. Boston: Beacon Press, 1928. ("Fantasy (Fancy)" reprinted in Boyer and Zahorski [29].)

160. Rose, Mark. *Alien Encounters: Anatomy of Science Fiction*. Cambridge, Mass.: Harvard University Press, 1981.

161. ———, ed. *Science Fiction: A Collection of Critical Essays*. Englewood Cliffs, N.J.: Prentice-Hall, 1976.

162. Rottensteiner, Franz. "European Theories of Fantasy," in Magill [127], vol. 5, pp. 2235–2246.

163. ———. *The Science Fiction Book: An Illustrated History*. New York: Seabury, 1975.

164. Russ, Joanna. "Dream Literature and Science Fiction." *Extrapolation* 11 (December 1969): 6–14.

165. ———. "Speculations: The Subjunctivity of Science Fiction." *Extrapolation* 15 (December 1973): 51–59.

166. ———. "Towards an Aesthetic of Science Fiction." *Science Fiction Studies* 2 (July 1975): 112–119.

167. Sale, Roger. *Fairy Tales and After: From Snow White to E. B. White*. Cambridge, Mass.: Harvard University Press, 1978.

168. Samuelson, David N. *Visions of Tomorrow: Six Journeys from Outer to Inner Space*. New York: Arno, 1974.

169. Schlobin, Roger C. "Fantasy versus Horror," in Magill [127], vol. 5, 2259–2265.

170. ———. *The Literature of Fantasy: A Comprehensive, Annotated Bibliography of Modern Fantasy Fiction*. New York: Garland, 1979.

171. ———, ed. *The Aesthetics of Fantasy Literature and Art*. Notre Dame: University of Notre Dame Press, 1982.

172. Schmerl, Rudolph B. "Fantasy as Technique." *Virginia Quarterly Review* 43 (Autumn 1967): 644–656. (Reprinted in Clareson [54].)

173. ———. "Reason's Dream: Anti-Totalitarian Themes and Techniques of Fantasy." *Dissertation Abstracts* 21 (1961): 2298.

174. Scholes, Robert. *Fabulation and Metafiction*. Urbana: University of Illinois Press, 1979.

175. ———. *The Fabulators*. New York: Oxford University Press, 1967.

176. ———. *Structural Fabulation: An Essay on Fiction of the Future*. Notre Dame, In.: University of Notre Dame Press, 1975.

177. ———. *Structuralism in Literature: An Introduction*. New Haven: Yale University Press, 1974.

178. ———, and Eric S. Rabkin. *Science Fiction: History, Science, Vision*. New York: Oxford University Press, 1977.

179. Searles, Baird, Martin Last, Beth Meachem, and Michael Franklin. *A Reader's Guide to Science Fiction*. New York: Avon, 1979.

180. Slusser, George E., Eric S. Rabkin, and Robert Scholes, eds. *Bridges to Fantasy*. Carbondale: Southern Illinois University Press, 1982.

181. ———, George R. Guffey, and Mark Rose, eds. *Bridges to Science Fiction*. Carbondale: Southern Illinois University Press, 1980.

182. ———, Eric S. Rabkin, and Robert Scholes, eds. *Coordinates: Placing Science Fiction and Fantasy*. Carbondale: Southern Illinois University Press, 1983.

183. Spencer, Kathleen L. " 'The Red Sun Is High, the Blue Low': Towards a Stylistic Description of Science Fiction." *Science Fiction Studies* 29 (March 1983): 35–49.

184. Spinrad, Norman. "On Books." *Destinies* 2, no. 3 (Summer 1980): 250–259.

185. Stableford, Brian. "The Mythology of Faerie," in Magill [127], vol. 5, pp. 2283–2298.

186. Suvin, Darko. "Narrative Logic, Ideological Domination, and the Range of SF: A Hypothesis with a Historical Test." *Science Fiction Studies* 26 (March 1982): 1–25.

187. ———. *Metamorphoses of Science Fiction: On the Poetics and History of a Literary Genre*. New Haven, Conn.: Yale University Press, 1979.

188. ———. *Victorian Science Fiction in the UK: The Discourses of Knowledge and of Power*. Boston: G.K. Hall, 1983.

189. Swinfen, Ann. *In Defence of Fantasy: A Study of the Genre in English and American Literature since 1945*. London: Routledge and Kegan Paul, 1984.

190. Thalmann, Marianne. *The Romantic Fairy Tale: Seeds of Surrealism*. trans. Mary B. Corcoran. Ann Arbor: University of Michigan Press, 1964.

191. Thompson, Hilary. "Doorways to Fantasy." *Canadian Children's Literature* 21 (1981): 8–16.

192. Thompson, Raymond H. "Arthurian Legend and Modern Fantasy," in Magill [127], vol. 5, pp. 2299–2315.

193. Todorov, Tzvetan. *The Fantastic: A Structural Approach to Literary Genre*. trans. Richard Howard. Ithaca, N.Y.: Cornell University Press, 1975.

194. Tolkien, J. R. R. "On Fairy-Stories." *Tree and Leaf*. London: Allen and Unwin, 1964. (Excerpt reprinted in Boyer & Zahorski [29].)

195. Touponce, William F. *Ray Bradbury and the Poetics of Reverie: Fantasy, Science Fiction, and the Reader*. Ann Arbor, Mich.: UMI Research Press, 1984.

196. Turner, George, and Peter Nicholls. "The SF Genealogy Scandal: An Exposé, with Cases for the Prosecution and Defence." *Foundation* 7–8 (March 1975): 159–176.

197. Tymn, Marshall B., Kenneth J. Zahorski, and Robert H. Boyer. *Fantasy Literature: A Core Collection and Reference Guide*. New York: R.R. Bowker, 1979.

198. Wagar, W. Warren. *Terminal Visions: The Literature of Last Things*. Bloomington: Indiana University Press, 1982.

199. Waggoner, Diana. *The Hills of Faraway: A Guide to Fantasy*. New York: Atheneum, 1978.

200. Walker, Jeanne Murray. "Myth, Exchange, and History in *The Left Hand of Darkness*." *Science Fiction Studies* 18 (July 1979): 180–189.

201. Warrick, Patricia. *The Cybernetic Imagination in Science Fiction*. Cambridge, Mass.: MIT Press, 1980.

202. Weinberg, Robert. "Fantasy Pulps," in Magill [127], vol. 5, pp. 2447–2463.

203. Wells, H. G. "Introduction." *Seven Famous Novels by H. G. Wells*. New York: Knopf, 1934.

204. Williamson, Jack, ed. *Teaching Science Fiction: Education for Tomorrow*. Philadelphia: Owlswick, 1980.

205. Wilson, Robin Scott. "The Terrific Play of Forces Natural and Human." In *Clarion*, ed. Robin Scott Wilson. New York: New American Library, 1971, pp. 203–212.

206. Wolfe, Gary K. "Contemporary Theories of Fantasy," in Magill [127], vol. 5, pp. 2220–2234.

207. ———. "The Encounter with Fantasy," in Schlobin [171].

208. ———. *The Known and the Unknown: The Iconography of Science Fiction*. Kent, Ohio: Kent State University Press, 1979.

209. ———. "Fairy Tales, *Märchen*, and Modern Fantasy," in Magill [127], vol. 5, pp. 2267–2281.

210. ———. "Symbolic Fantasy." *Genre* 8, no. 3 (September 1975): 194–209.

211. Wolfe, Gene. "What Do They Mean, SF?" *SFWA Bulletin* no. 75 (1981): 20–25.

212. Wollheim, Donald A. *The Universe Makers: Science Fiction Today*. New York: Harper, 1971.

213. Yolen, Jane. *Touch Magic: Fantasy, Faerie and Folklore in the Literature of Childhood*. New York: Philomel, 1981.

214. Zanger, Jules. "Heroic Fantasy and Social Reality: *ex nihilo nihil fit*," in Schlobin [171].

215. Zgorzelski, Andrzej. "Is Science Fiction a Genre of Fantastic Literature?" *Science Fiction Studies* 19 (November 1979): 296–303.

216. Ziolkowski, Theodore. *Disenchanted Images: A Literary Iconology*. Princeton, N.J.: Princeton University Press, 1977.

217. Zipes, Jack. *Breaking the Magic Spell: Radical Theories of Folk and Fairy Tales*. Austin: University of Texas Press, 1979.

218. ———. *Fairy Tales and the Art of Subversion: The Classical Genre for Children and the Process of Civilization*. New York: Wildman Press, 1983.

Index of Primary Authors

This index contains citations of fiction authors used as examples in the text. It does not include critics or critical writings, since these are listed in the bibliography and cited individually in each entry.

About the Author

GARY K. WOLFE is Dean of the Evelyn T. Stone College of Continuing Education at Roosevelt University. He is the author of *The Known and the Unknown: The Iconography of Science Fiction* and is a frequent contributor to periodicals, critical anthologies, and reference works on science fiction and related subjects.